STAYING RELEVANT

STAYING RELEVANT

SAM THOMPSON & PETE WICKS

SPHERE

SPHERE

First published in Great Britain in 2025 by Sphere

1 3 5 7 9 10 8 6 4 2

Copyright © Staying Relevant Productions Limited 2025

The moral right of the authors has been asserted.

All rights reserved.
No part of this publication may be reproduced, stored in a retrieval system, or transmitted, in any form or by any means, without the prior permission in writing of the publisher, nor be otherwise circulated in any form of binding or cover other than that in which it is published and without a similar condition including this condition being imposed on the subsequent purchaser.

A CIP catalogue record for this book
is available from the British Library.

ISBN 978-1-4087-3474-2

Typeset in Warnock by M Rules
Printed and bound in Great Britain by
Clays Ltd, Elcograf S.p.A.

Papers used by Sphere are from well-managed forests
and other responsible sources.

MIX
Paper | Supporting
responsible forestry
FSC
www.fsc.org FSC® C104740

Sphere
An imprint of
Little, Brown Book Group
Carmelite House
50 Victoria Embankment
London EC4Y 0DZ

The authorised representative
in the EEA is
Hachette Ireland
8 Castlecourt Centre
Dublin 15, D15 XTP3, Ireland
(email: info@hbgi.ie)

An Hachette UK Company
www.hachette.co.uk

www.littlebrown.co.uk

To our *Staying Relevant* team, fans and family.
Thank you for always being there for us.
We love you.

CONTENTS

Brainstorming   1

PART 1
IRRELEVANT

1. When Will I Be Famous?   21
2. Baby Steps Towards Fame   29
3. Dating and Drama = Relevance   52
4. The Public React   57
5. Personal Appearances   65

PART 2
ALMOST RELEVANT

6. Next Steps   81
7. Money is Relevant   88
8. Building Your Brand   92
9. Building Your Brand Part 2   99

10.	Getting Noticed	110
11.	Imposter Syndrome	115
12.	Divas	122

PART 3
BECOMING RELEVANT

13.	When Sam Met Pete	135
14.	Can't Fight the Chemistry	161
15.	*Staying Relevant* Begins	163
16.	Doing It Ourselves	183
17.	Behind the Scenes of *Staying Relevant*	193

PART 4
WHAT COMES WITH RELEVANCE

18.	The Dark Art of Social Media	209
19.	Fandom	224
20.	When Being a Celebrity Changes Other People's Lives	228
21.	The Reality of Reality	237
22.	Dating in the Public Eye	255
23.	Getting the Look	272
24.	The Benefits of Fame	283

PART 5
STAYING RELEVANT

25.	Going Legit	293
26.	Going Legit Part 2	314
27.	The Importance of Having Proper Mates	342
28.	Staying Resilient	348
	The Future	357
	Acknowledgements	367

Brainstorming

April 2025. A central London café.

Sam
Welcome to *Staying Relevant*, a book written by two best friends: me, Samuel Robert De Courcy Thompson, and Peter James Joseph *Quentin* Wicks.

Pete
Quentin? For fuck's sake, another fake name? Anyway... as you already know from our podcast...

Sam
Our insanely successful and *award-winning* podcast.

Pete
... there will be swearing. So much swearing, in fact, that if you don't like it, you can go fuck yourself. I haven't been drinking much lately, but, as you can imagine, hanging out with this fucking bellend during the writing of this book has driven me right back to the booze. Which might explain some of the shit that comes out of my mouth. I strongly suggest you have a drink or two yourselves – it might help you get through the next eighty thousand words.

Sam

Eighty thousand words? Wow, that's a lot.

Pete

It is, Sam. Which is why you'll find I'll be doing most of the fucking talking, while this gobby tit floats off into his dream world, thinking up more cringey TikToks to embarrass me with ... while taking most of the credit for the fucking book – *and* half the money the publisher has stupidly given us to write this!

Sam

And here we are! I've got my quill in my hand, my notebook at the ready. I'm raring to go! I mean, this is awesome. A book, Pete! We're writing a fucking book!

Pete

Well, it ain't my first rodeo. Let's not forget my *Sunday Times* bestseller *Never Enough* – still available to buy, by the way – and *For the Love of Frenchies* from 2018. But yes, this is our first – and most probably our last – foray into the publishing world together.

Sam

I can't believe it, mate. I can't wait to read it.

Pete

Well, we have to write it first.

Sam

Er, hang on ... We have, though, haven't we? That's what our *Staying Relevant* family are holding in their hands right now?

Pete
Well, yeah, it is *now* ... but technically, we hadn't written shit when we did this bit. And to break the fourth wall for a minute – just to clarify for you poor sods who've forked out for this – what you're currently reading is a stream of consciousness from months ago. Way before we even properly started writing. Picture this: an empty central London café at 11 a.m., a very tired me just off air from presenting Kiss FM's breakfast show with my mate Olivia Attwood ...

Sam
Ah, the third glorious wheel in our beautiful relationship!

Pete
Yep. My favourite third, as it happens. Anyway, this is the first time we're actually getting round to talking about what the book is going to be about.

Sam
Ooh, I'd better get comfortable then.

Pete
Comfortable? This isn't a fucking therapy session. It's work!

Sam
I just feel like I'm all hunched up, leaning into the phone.

Pete
Well, let's lean back then, shall we?

Sam
Ah, that's better. Feet on the table? Or is that too much?

Pete

Too much. Always too much. We're in a café. You're not at home.

Sam

So ... what's the book about?

Pete

Cross-stitch! What do you think it's about, you prick? It's a *Staying Relevant* book. It's about fame – and the desperate, humiliating, soul-destroying lengths you and I have gone to, to achieve it and maintain it.

Sam

So, you're saying this is like a handy guide for people who want to follow in our footsteps and find out more about us along the way?

Pete

No. One thing this is not is a guide on how to become the next big Z-lister. Only a proper cunt would come up with an idea like that.

Sam

So it's like the *Staying Relevant* quest for fame! Because being famous is sooo awesome! It's the BEST!

Pete

And this is why this book might actually be pretty good. You see, Sam thinks being famous is the bollocks.

Sam

It is! It's the absolute bollocks. Big hairy, bulbous bollocks, full of juicy goodness.

Pete
While I think fame is as much fun as having to sit through a twenty-four-hour marathon of your least favourite TV show.

Sam
Which means fame is fucking awesome!

Pete
Anyway ... let's get moving, otherwise this book is going to be a thousand pages long. And I'm already getting bored as fuck.

Sam
Okay, so how should the book start?

Pete
Well, the pod started because of our quest to be famous, so why don't we start with fame and the days before we were relevant?

Sam
Are we famous? That is the question. Are we? *Are we?*

Pete
Well, what does 'being famous' mean?

Sam
I think 'being famous' is getting let into nightclubs for free.

Pete
Jesus Christ. That's one of the most pathetic things I've ever heard.

Sam
That's the entire reason I joined *Made in Chelsea*.

Pete
How fucking sad. I used to get into nightclubs for free because I actually knew people.

Sam
You see, I didn't. I got bounced even when I was twenty-one.

Pete
Yeah, and at twenty-one you looked like a sewer rat.

Sam
And I looked about fifteen.

Pete
To be fair, you still actually look young, while I look like I've been knocking around for donkey's years. Stupid question, I know, but would you say you're happy being famous?

Sam
Fuck yeah, mate! Are you joking? It's the best in the world.

Pete
I fucking hate it.

Sam
I know you hate it – everyone knows you hate it – because you don't like people. I absolutely love people. Do you know what? There is nothing better – literally nothing better – in the world than someone you don't know coming up to talk to you.

Pete

Well, it depends, really, because I've had people I don't know come up and call me a cunt. So that's not so great, is it?

Sam

I love it. When guys in a van drive past me and yell, 'You're that funny cunt from thingy!' I love it. I'm like, 'Yes! Come on!'

Pete

That's true. There's been times at PAs...

Sam

That's personal appearances, for those who aren't sure.

Pete

Sam, our readers know what a PA is. They've been listening to the pod for three fucking years.

Sam

But what if someone reading this hasn't listened to *Staying Relevant* before, and bought it because they'd seen me on *Made in Chelsea* or *I'm a Celeb*, or you getting with a babe on *TOWIE*, or shaking your arse on *Strictly*?

Pete

Then they must be out of their minds. Buying a book based on a podcast they haven't listened to – who does that? They must have more money than sense. Anyway, where was I before you chipped in with your scat chat?

But we thank you anyway – Sam

Sam

PAs. Personal appearances.

Pete
Oh yeah. You see, Sam will literally do anything any fucker asks him to.

Sam
I do. I can't deny it. I'm a people-pleaser.

Pete
So, let's get back to it. We'll leave the whole concept of fame on the back burner. Why are *we* actually doing the book?

Sam
I haven't got a clue. You just told me we were doing it. I was like, 'Okay, sweet. We're doing a book. Great.'

Pete
Fuck me. Well, this book, for me, is a look back at the madness of the past decade of us trying to stay relevant. Even though I've hated every single fucking minute of it.

That's not entirely true – Pete

Sam
Are we gonna go deep?

Pete
Well, I'm almost forty fucking years old, so yeah – I'm going to give it a good go. I want to write about some of the big things, proper things, rather than just talking about getting into scraps with geezers or you getting picked up like a fish.

Sam
Awesome! Let's get balls deep. I'm totally ready. Two-footed, straight in.

Pete
So I'd say this is a chance for us to reflect on how we

became Sam and Pete, this weird little duo that, for some reason, people seem to like.

Sam
You mean millions of people. We're bloody superstars, Pete.

Pete
Get back in your box.

Sam
But we are! We're Beyoncé. We're Adele. We're Ed fucking Sheeran. We just played the O2! We're rock stars, mate.

Pete
Remember, this is being written in the spring of 2025, so hopefully the show wasn't cancelled because one of us got killed during one of Sam's dumb TikToks.

Anyway, back to why we're doing the book. I still can't get my head around it. For some baffling reason, the public have really got behind us, for which I'm genuinely grateful. I mean, if someone wants to think the sun shines out of my arse, who am I to stop them? I'm not entirely sure what that says about the great British public – probably that they're clinically insane – but I'll take it.

Sam
A win's a win! I love the public. They're awesome. *Staying Relevant* fam – we fucking love you.

Pete
But Sam, you always imagined this life. This was never my plan. So I reckon we're going to delve deep into what we both wanted out of our lives and how we ended up where we are. I mean, without you, I wouldn't be here, hosting podcasts, writing books, getting dicked up against walls

dressed as fucking Spider-Man. And I hate you for that. I really fucking do. All this is really about you. I just get dragged along for the ride. I'm a side dish, the garlic bread – not filling enough for a main. You're the main course.

He doesn't really

Sam
Yeah, like a big cheesy pizza with meat toppings and extra spice. The one that gives you ring sting.

Pete
Jesus, we're getting paid to write this shit. How the fuck did I get here? I ask myself that daily, usually after spending three hours dancing around like a twat in an inflatable outfit at Sam's house. You'd never believe I used to have a proper job. In an office. This batshit crazy world was never a thought in my mind. Whereas you, Sam – you always wanted this.

Sam
I did. And I love it. And we've worked hard for it.

Pete
But has it been worth it? Has fame turned out the way you thought it would?

Sam
You know what? I don't think so ... and let me tell you why.

Pete
I can't wait for this earth-shattering revelation.

Sam
Because I never think we've made it.

Pete
Because we fucking haven't!

Sam
Exactly. People tell us we have – that we've done this, that, whatever – but I'm like, 'I don't feel like we have.'

Pete
In fairness, the only people saying we've made it are the ones fresh off a reality show, doing their first PAs. Give it two years and we'll be asking them if we can appear on their show. 'If you need someone to do a voiceover ...'

That's the circle of reality life

Sam
Yep, we're your guys. I genuinely don't think we've made it. It's weird, because I always think back to when I was in the jungle ...

Pete
He can't get enough of telling us he was on that! That's mention number two!

Sam
You go in there and you're surrounded by actual famous people. Properly famous. And I've always wanted to be one of them. But I still don't think we will be.

Pete
Well, that's what this book is about. We're going to explore the nature of fame – why people chase it, how we found ourselves stuck in it – look back at all the crazy shit we've done, and cringe at all the stuff we've had to do to stay in the public eye and earn a few quid. Plus, like any good story, there'll be drama as we look back at bad relationships and fall-outs ...

Sam
And lashings of bromance as we open up about our very special friendship and what we really mean to each other.

Pete
I can tell you right now, Sam: fuck all. Right, my coffee's cold and I'm knackered. I'm heading back to my flat to see my dogs and have a well-earned kip. From here on in, you can enjoy – well, that might be a stretch – the book we've been talking about. And if you get bored, why not make a note of all the times I say 'fuck' or 'cunt'? That'll keep you on your toes.

Ten minutes later.

Pete
Right, I'm back at my pad, dogs by my side. After that absolute car crash of an opener, I'm taking the reins for a bit to salvage whatever's left of this shitshow. Let's get one thing straight: this book is just two fucking idiots spouting opinions and banging on about the completely random jobs we did to get to where we are, and trying to finally work out how this fucking weird and occasionally dysfunctional friendship came into being and why it's lasted so long.

So don't come here expecting *War and* fucking *Peace*. This is the sort of thing you read on the bog while having a shit – or better yet, wipe your arse with afterwards.

Oh Pete, there will be lots of them. Go grab a tissue!

If you're after some literary masterpiece, shut this book now and walk away. And if you're expecting anything even close to the heart-wrenching, emotional rollercoaster of my last book – which, by the way, I actually *did* pour my heart and soul into – then prepare to be monumentally disappointed. There'll be no tears here. No vulnerability. Just swearing, and some serious frustration (mainly directed at Sam). What you can look forward to in this mess is me having a good old rant about some prick from the past, while Dopey fucking Drawers pipes up every five minutes, going on about how much he wants to hug people.

Let's be honest – the main reason Sam and I are doing this isn't just the lovely pay packet (although that does help). It's because, for some sick, twisted reason, people are intrigued by our friendship. And it's a weird one, I'll give you that. I've never loved and hated someone in such equal measure. They say there's a fine line between love and hate – and with us, that line is damn fine.

It's a proper odd-couple dynamic: two people who, without fame, would never have crossed paths. People seem to love seeing us be mates – probably because you couldn't get more chalk and cheese than me and Sam.

We met on TV – we're not old schoolmates. I barely went to school, while Sam had bloody Jeeves the butler dropping him off at his fancy boarding school's gates. Now that I've known him ten years, I totally get why his family packed him off at age seven. Who the fuck would want to live with him? They probably had his suitcase ready before he stopped shitting in nappies. And if I could send him away now? I'd do it in a heartbeat.

Sorry mate, I'm stuck to you like glue!

MAYBE THE BEST THING THAT HAPPENED TO US IS WE FOUND EACH OTHER

Pete

See what Anna Williamson says about our 'bromance' in Chapter 13

On paper – and in life – what Sam and I have is the most unlikely of friendships. And yet, weirdly, it's probably the only successful relationship to ever come out of Celebs Go Dating. If we hadn't been a pair of social-climbing reality stars who met on that show, we'd never have crossed paths. We wouldn't have started a successful business together. We wouldn't have launched a podcast – a podcast, I might add, that I didn't even want to do.

Sam had to convince me. I had zero interest. I genuinely didn't think anyone would give a shit about what two wallies like us had to say about anything. But – and it fucking pains me to admit this – he was right. *Staying Relevant* has somehow turned into this thing that's kind of like our baby. A massive, weird, ugly baby, granted, but one we've grown to love anyway.

In fact, I'd go as far as to say the podcast is probably what we're most proud of. Out of everything we've done. Between us, we've pretty much completed reality TV. There isn't a show we haven't touched – and that's purely because we'll do anything for money. We have no shame. Someone says 'do it', we do it. Sam fucking loves all that. Without TV and without fame, he'd probably still be working in a bar ... or living off Daddy's money.

Me? I'm the opposite. This whole ride has left me with a confusing sense of purpose. People always want to know what our day-to-day looks like. And when you're on TV or in the public eye, they assume it's all really fucking easy. And look – we are lucky. We know that. But it's been a slog. Over a decade of graft. We both started around the same time, scrapping around with all the other aspiring arseholes desperately trying to make a living.

And maybe the best thing that ever happened to us is that we found each other. Why? Because since that moment, we've both gone on to do all sorts of mad shit.

Sam

Like appearing on the country's biggest TV shows, meeting amazing people like the king of fucking England, His Majesty King Charles and George Clooney, working with brilliant charities like UNICEF and making loads of dosh for doing ads for big brands like Subway and Burger King.

Technically that was just you, Sam

Pete

We even had our own show. It got cancelled – probably because I said 'cunt' too much. So I've learned from that, tried to tone it down. Although I've just said 'cunt' twice in the last ten seconds, so maybe not a great start.

But yeah, we teamed up to try and actually make a proper go of this whole fucking game together.

And at the risk of sounding like a right soppy twat, it has been a beautiful thing, sharing this journey. A journey I never thought I'd be on. I mean, I thought I'd have a proper job by now. Some self-respect. Bit of dignity. Instead, here I am – just fucking Sam Thompson's mate. It's a sad existence, but it's mine. So I deal with it.

Thing is, I reckon both Sam and I want to share our lives with people – and not in the scripted way. That stuff's not 'reality' any more. Not really. What we want to do is give you a proper glimpse of what our lives actually look like. The madness of it. The chaos. The stuff that makes us feel lucky, and the stuff that makes us question everything.

And the easiest way to do that? Put it all in a book. You know what I mean? Lay it bare, so people can try and understand just how fucking strange – and strangely brilliant – this ride has been.

I actually think writing this book might end up being quite cathartic for me. A bit of therapy, really, trying to work out how the fuck we're still friends. Maybe that's it. The last book I wrote made me re-evaluate my life a little bit ... Maybe this one will give me some answers too. Like: why is Sam Thompson my friend?

So yes – this book will be fun, probably quite insightful for you lot, but it's also a journey of discovery for me. And the big question is: should I finally dump him, or keep him around a bit longer? By the end of this book, we'll either be stronger than ever ... or this'll be the last thing we do together. Who knows? We'll find out together.

And if you think you know us already, you're wrong. You're gonna find out a hell of a lot about me and Sam. Probably more than you ever needed or wanted to know, to be honest. I learn new shit about him every day. But I reckon – spoiler alert – the biggest takeaway from all this is that we are as normal as it gets.

Boring, I know. But that's kind of the point. This book isn't about the glossy, filtered version of us that people think they know. It's about the real Sam and Pete, the ones behind the nonsense. The ones who wake up, have a shit, have a shave and just get on with life like everyone else.

Because here's the thing: just because we've made tits of ourselves on TV, people act like we're somehow special. Like we're bloody gods made of solid gold. There's this perception that being famous sets you apart from the rest of the world. But that's bollocks. Anyone could do what we do.

We get paid to be ourselves. We don't have any talent. Not a single fucking ounce of it between us. There's nothing Sam or I are actually good at. *Nothing.* And yet people stop us in the street for photos or send us weird shit in the post. Why? We're just two wallies, one who looks like he's crawled out of a wheelie bin and the other who no one noticed until he got his teeth done. Snaggletooth Thompson and the fucking hairy cunt. That's us.

And as I write this, it's dawning on me that maybe this book is really just about us trying to understand why we are where we are.

Reality stars get a bad rap. And to be fair, some of them fucking deserve it. There's a right load of tits out there. But are we really any different? I don't know. I do respect anyone who puts themselves out there to try and better their life. That's usually the reason people get into this – to change something, to reach for something more. Everyone's reasons are different. Some crave the limelight. Others, like me, never wanted it. I was just looking for a new experience and didn't really think about what came with it. I'm actually quite private. I like being private. I miss the days when I could just disappear. Fade into nothingness. That's harder to do now.

If someone asked me what superpower I'd have, I wouldn't say flying or strength or any of that bollocks. I'd say invisibility. Without question. I'd fucking love to be invisible. Sam, on the other hand, loves the spotlight, the attention, the validation, all of it. Maybe he didn't get all that growing up. Maybe he wasn't the most popular kid. And now he's found a way to fill that gap.

In a way, that kind of validation, that love from people, is a beautiful thing. I never really gave a fuck what people thought. But weirdly, doing this job has made me care more than I ever did. But probably for all the wrong reasons.

Because now, you get these heartfelt messages from people. Lovely stuff. And suddenly it gives you this weird sense of responsibility – like you can't let people down. And that's one of my biggest fears: letting people down. But it's not just your mum or your mates any more.

There's this whole army of people, whether it's the O2 crowd or the podcast listeners, and if we do a shit episode I sit there thinking, I've let them all down. And then I'm like, Why do I even care? I don't know them! Those silly fuckers aren't my problem.

But ... I do care. You feel this pressure to always be at your best. To deliver. And that's hard. That's fucking hard.

So there you go. That's the manifesto for this book. Now grab a bevvy, get comfy and take a little trip down memory lane with us – through the best bits, the worst bits, and all the absolute bottom-of-the-barrel moments in between.

And help me figure out, by the end of this book, whether Sam and I should still be mates.

The choice is yours.

Part 1

Irrelevant

1

When Will I Be Famous?

Why the fuck would you wanna be?

Sam

So, let's start at the very beginning of our story, long before Pete and I were what you'd even dare to call famous. Back in the distant past when the idea of writing a book like this wasn't even a consideration. Those were the days when our *Staying Relevant* story actually began, though we certainly didn't realise it at the time.

Pete

If you think about it, it's pretty mad where Sam and I are these days. Who'd have thought some posh kid from Chelsea and a long-haired gobby lad would one day form a friendship that would ultimately change their lives? I can't help but wonder, if we hadn't started doing what we did eleven years ago would we be the people we are today? What impact has fame had on who we've become? Has it made us better people ... or worse?

Wow, we're getting deep already

For me, I think it's probably made me a better person — mostly because every mistake I've ever made (and trust me, there's been a fuckload) has been documented, dissected and scrutinised. I've had to face up to every part of myself that's a complete dickhead — which, let's be honest, is the majority of me. You don't get to fuck up quietly. It hasn't stopped me, but if I hadn't been in the public eye, maybe I'd have just carried on down that same road – mullet and all – without ever looking back.

I NEVER WANTED FAME IN THE FIRST PLACE

Pete

When I look back at my pre-fame days ... I think I was a bit of a prick.

A little bit selfish. I still can be, to be honest – but can't we all? Probably why I'm still single. I'm too selfish, too ambitious, too caught up in my own shit to let someone else in. I used to have a very small-minded view of life. I knew exactly where I wanted to go and what I wanted to do, and I didn't want help. Didn't accept guidance. Just tunnel vision.

Before I was acting like a prat on *TOWIE*, I was the international sales director for a medical recruitment company. Can you believe it? Me – with a full-time job, doing actual grown-up stuff. And I was pretty good at it too. I made sure only the best of the best doctors ended up in the right places. At one point, I even considered starting my own recruitment agency. The plan was: build it up, sell it for millions then move into capital investment. That was it. The vision. I wanted to be retired by forty. Settled. Sorted. Now I'm thirty-seven and still living like a fucking eighteen-year-old. It's wild.

Do I miss it? Yeah, probably. Why? For the security. The control. I'm a control freak, which will come as no surprise to anyone who even half knows me.

But when I fell into this world I started to see all the great things I could do. And now, all these years later, I've achieved so much and my whole view of life has changed. After years of moaning about not really feeling part of the showbiz world, I discovered I was pretty good at it and found myself on a career path I never thought I'd be on. I mean, who'd have thought that Pirate Pete would end up running his own production company?

I WAS RIPPED FROM MY MOTHER'S ARMS AND SENT TO BOARDING SCHOOL

Sam

There are two reasons why I wanted to do reality TV when I was younger. First of all, I wanted to do it for the most ridiculous and selfish reasons – to get into nightclubs, have some drinks and get with girls. A pretty basic and embarrassing reason, I agree, but when you're a gawky, not-exactly-great-looking teenager, you look for any way you can to make life better.

Good point

Pete
No arguments from me!

Sam

I needed my ego massaged, and for me, that was reality TV, mainly because I'd seen my sister's life change for the better when she joined the cast of *Made in Chelsea*, the scripted reality show that wasn't *The Only Way is Essex*!

Pete
The snooty one where everyone strutted along the streets of west London necking champagne.

Sam

Even though Lou got emotionally battered when she was dating on the show, she reaped the rewards of being on telly: getting invited to parties and events, hanging out with famous people and making money from flogging stuff online.

I was a bit of a tyke at school, but I only ever got in

trouble with the police once, when I tried to crash a bar called Amika on Kensington High Street with fake ID. See – as a spotty teenager, I was pretty desperate to get into a club!

What a criminal mastermin[d]. Bet the Kr[ay] twins wer[e] quaking i[n] their boot[s].

Pete
Fuck me, I guess in Chelsea they're not fighting the same kind of crimes they do down in Essex!

Sam
For some mad reason, the police were called and two officers actually escorted me all the way home. I was shitting myself, but when my mum answered the door she was like, 'Oh my lord, what's he done?' When they told her I'd been caught with fake ID, she just laughed and said, 'Really? Is that it?'

Pete
Karen is one top girl.

Sam
When I was about seven, I was sent to a boarding school in the country called Horris Hill.

Pete
Ah, so your mum had had enough of you by this point. Understandable.

Sam
I have to admit, it felt a bit like I was being ripped away from home. It was tough. I remember when my mum dropped me off, she started crying. Then when the reality of not going back home hit me, I started bawling too.

Luckily, I got used to it super quickly, once I got in with a group of mates. In the end, it was brilliant. I loved it: the sport, the banter, everything. I was basically a sportsman, never an academic. I was in all the first teams – rugby, football, cricket. I cared about my mates, the fun of it all.

I LOST MY VIRGINITY, THREW MY HANDS IN THE AIR AND SCREAMED 'YEEEEAAAAH!'

Sam
My secondary boarding school – Bradfield College, near Reading – was co-ed, and it was where I got to mix with girls for the first time. I was like, Wow. Okay. Game on.

Pete
Jesus, I bet they weren't prepared for Hurricane fucking Sam!

Sam
Actually, no. To start with, I was super nervous. I didn't talk to any of them – just watched them . . .

Pete
You what?

Sam
In a non-creepy way.

Pete
Is there such a thing?

Sam
You can see now why being famous was such a goal for me!

Pete
Yeah, so you could become someone who wasn't you!

Sam

Then, when I got a bit of confidence, the lads and I would try and sneak into their dorms. We'd throw pebbles at the windows, but they'd just tell us to go home.

My first proper crush was a girl called Georgia Rose. Big crush. But I was just her mate. No one knew I fancied her. I actually thought I *loved* her. All my mates would ask her out, and I'd just sit there thinking, God, I'd love to, but I don't have the courage.

Pete

Not surprised, but these things happen.

Sam

What are you saying – you went through the same thing?

Pete

Course not. I was fine, thanks. I was talking more about guys like you: awkward, gamer, online mates.

Sam

I was a bit of a handful and got up to all sorts, but somehow I always managed to get away with it, while everyone else was getting suspended or expelled. That said, I did get suspended four times.

Pete

Rebel!

Sam

But my teachers all seemed to like me. They always saw me as the unlucky guy who just happened to be in the wrong place at the wrong time.

Pete
Yeah, I felt like that when we met for the first time.

Sam
I think they saw potential in me, because they'd always say things like, 'Look, we know you're trying to be a good lad, you're just a bit of an idiot sometimes.' So I kind of always managed to wriggle out of it.

Academically, I was rubbish. I was good at English literature, and when I know I'm good at something I try to excel at it. But with something I'm not good at – like maths – I don't even try. I'd look at the board, see numbers and my brain would just shut down. But when I've got a passion for something – like creating content for social media – I thrive off encouragement. If my housemaster told me my homework was brilliant, I'd run back and do something else for him. But if no one showed interest, I'd just think, fuck it, and go find something else to do.

Pete
Fuck me, you're a needy knob. Now, shut up and get back to your boring fucking school story,

Sam
I probably would've been all right at academics if I'd applied myself more. But yeah, English lit was the one for me. I got an A. Of course, back then I didn't know I had ADHD. I'd only find that out in my thirties. I wonder how different things would have been if I knew then what I know now.

For A levels I did photography and history of art, mainly to talk to girls. But none of them fancied me. I was the only boy in the class so there was no competition, and still nothing. I ended up being friends with all of them, but I didn't go out with anyone.

I lost my virginity at fifteen to a lovely girl from school. We were at a house party, and it just happened. We did it in my mate's mum's wardrobe. Then I literally ran out, threw my hands in the air and went *'Yeeeeaaaah!'*

2

Baby Steps Towards Fame

Way back in the 2010s, reality TV exploded. **TOWIE and** Made in Chelsea *turned everyday Brits into tabloid royalty.*

Pete
Before I joined *TOWIE*, I didn't have a fucking clue about reality TV.

I didn't watch it, didn't pay much attention to it, but I knew it was out there, mainly 'cos my mate James 'Lockie' Lock was part of it. I also knew I hated it. I thought it was full of absolute jokers who spent their time getting fake tans and lip fillers. Anyway, the idea of ever ending up on a show like *TOWIE* had never even crossed my mind. Until, that is, I was approached by the producers at Sheesh restaurant in Essex on a night out with Lockie. At first, I was like, 'Fuck off – that's the last thing I wanna do.' But work was starting to get on my tits, and after thinking about it I figured it might be a laugh – take my mind off things for a bit.

Sam
A change is as good as a rest! Even if it's on reality telly with your life playing out in front of millions!

Pete
So I met with the producers. They liked what they saw and asked me to 'come and do a couple of eps'. Just a fleeting cameo. In and out. Easy. Next thing I know, I'm flown out to fucking Marbella and told to get myself to some villa party where, let's just say, I turned a few heads. And to cut a long story short (or read it in fuller detail in my book *Never Enough*) I became a bit of thing in the press.

BEFORE I'D EVEN AIRED, I WAS SPLASHED ALL OVER THE TABLOIDS

Pete
The filming side of it didn't bother me. I felt pretty chilled, to be honest. I wasn't taking it seriously – just having a laugh. But I could tell everyone was curious about me, asking each other who I was. I liked that. Ruffled a few feathers. Didn't faze me, though – none of them were my mates, so I didn't give a toss what they thought.

But as soon as I shot my first scene, everything went a bit mad. Word got out that some new bloke had joined the cast – long hair, covered in tatts, blue eyes, not your standard *TOWIE* geezer. The papers lapped it up. Before I'd even aired, I was splashed all over the tabloids. And that's when it got even crazier. Out of nowhere, I started getting messages from people asking me to do appearances at their clubs – offering me a grand just to turn up.

Sam
You lucky bastard. I got diddly squat!

Pete
I bit their hands off. I was doing PAs before I'd even been on TV. What a result. At the time, I didn't have a manager. I didn't think I needed one as I was only meant to be doing

a few episodes out in Marbella, then back to my normal life – my boring, unglamorous but safe and well-paid day job. Who'd have thought I'd spend the next decade or so actually trying to stay in the game! And ultimately succeed.

A PRODUCER'S DREAM – AND THEIR WORST FUCKING NIGHTMARE

Pete
It didn't take long for me to get into the swing of things on *TOWIE*. I actually started to enjoy the filming process, but didn't feel totally invested in it. Not at that point, anyway. I thought to myself, if people liked it, great. If they didn't, I didn't give a fuck. That's just how I am – I wasn't nervous, I wasn't scared, never have been.

Sam
Well of course you weren't. You're Peter James Wicks – they were probably scared of *you*! But I reckon they loved you. You're a producer's dream!

Pete
And their worst fucking nightmare.

Sam
Oh I bet, but from what I know of you, you get the job done!

Pete
I went in thinking, I'm not gonna be told what to say or do. I was just gonna be real – take it or leave it. And over time, I learned that even though it's called 'reality', what you see on camera ain't always the full story. There's plenty that goes on behind the scenes that you don't see. And some of the cast were really lovely people – beautiful inside and out.

Sam

I know we moan about our reality pasts sometimes – well, Pete has on more than one occasion – but a lot of the time the rest of the cast were great.

Pete

They couldn't believe their luck. They were getting paid to be on holiday, film a few bits, go out, live it up. What a life. And we knew how lucky we were. Everyone was mates, genuinely. It wasn't just work. We'd all go out together, have a laugh, proper camaraderie. That was reality TV back then. Different world.

I THOUGHT DOING THE SHOW WAS GOING TO BE A PIECE OF PISS, BUT ON MY FIRST DAY I JUST PANICKED

Sam

Meanwhile on the other side of London, I was desperate to be part of reality TV, as you know. I'd seen my sister have great time on *Made in Chelsea* and wanted a piece of the pie myself so could live life as a king, get into as many swanky bars as I could and maybe, just maybe, get with a girl or two!

Pete

Yeah, so you keep telling us. What aspirations! You get more tragic by the minute.

Sam

I was super young, mate. I wanted to live the life. By this stage I'd left school and gone to Australia on a gap year, where I'd planned to stay for seven months and do the whole Gold Coast, then fuck off to Thailand. But I loved Sydney so much I got lost in it and started thinking, Shit, I could live here for the rest of my life. But then my visa ran out, so I couldn't. So I came back to London and got myself a job at Broadway House in Fulham, as front of house for its members' bar. Easiest job I've ever done. Checking and swiping membership cards. I basically watched *Frozen Planet* every single night and got a kebab on the way home. That was it.

Pete
Good to see you took your job seriously as always!

Sam
Then one day these two women came in, called Roz and Sarah, who had just been to the *Made in Chelsea* end-of-season party. Turns out they were producers of the show. I got excited and squealed, 'I'm Louise's brother.' And they were like, 'Really? That's interesting.' I can't tell if they were really interested or just humouring me, but they gave me their number anyway and said, 'Give us a call.' Result! I thought. No more work. I was suddenly excited! I would get to meet girls as part of my job! What more could I ask for? I didn't waste any time and called them the next day, but sadly it didn't work out that time.

Pete
Why? 'Cos they could tell you were a twat?

Sam
Probably. But they said I looked so young. I was twenty, but I looked about eighteen. And they didn't think I was going to hook up with anyone.

Pete
Rough! But fucking true. I mean, who would wanna snog Snaggletooth?

Sam
Yes, I agree, I was orally challenged.

Pete
In many ways!

Sam
Looking back, I can see why they were unsure about me. I mean, the show is predominantly about dating, and it would have been stupid for me to have gone on at that point because – sadly – there was no danger of me becoming *MiC*'s resident lothario. So I carried on working at Broadway House, saved a bit of money and took half a year out to enjoy life and party while I was young.

Then later that summer, I bumped into Sarah and Roz again in a beer garden. I looked a little bit older and was with a big group of people.

Pete
Were the gnashers any better?

Sam
Sadly not – they would come in time – but it didn't seem to put them off. They gingerly said to me, 'Oh, we're casting for the show.' I reminded them that I was Louise's brother, and they seemed shocked – 'Oh my God, yeah. You look so different' – and asked me to come on the show. Louise was going out with a lovely guy called Andy Jordan, and because they were experiencing a few ups and downs in their relationship, she was getting a lot of screen time and they thought I could easily fit into the show. I told them I knew other cast members (I didn't) and that I had opinions on everything, and tried to make myself sound like I was going to be the next big thing on the show. As it turned out, I wasn't.

Pete

No you weren't, were you? Fuck me, could our lives be any more different? There's me coming in an accidental instant hit with viewers on *TOWIE*, and there's you sloping unnoticed in as Snaggletooth the drippy extra.

Sam

I wasn't Snaggletooth. In the early days I was referred to on-screen as 'Louise's brother'.

Pete

Oh yeah, that's right, you weren't even named for the first six months, were you? You were just 'Louise's brother'!

Sam

I had a tough time settling in. I thought doing the show was going to be a piece of piss. But on my first day I just panicked, got a bit of stage fright and ended up doing fifteen takes of my first scene.

Pete

Fifteen fucking takes? How? It's *reality* TV. What happens just happens. You *never* have to do things over and over again.

Sam

I stacked it. I got nervous.

Pete

I guess that's the major difference between the two of us. You do fifteen takes of the same scene, while I rock up, film a scene then hobble off to the bar.

Sam

It wasn't even meant to be my scene. My sister was getting dumped by Andy. All I had to do was open the door for him. But by the fifteenth take he ended up walking *me* into my own house because I'd fucked it up so many times. He felt sorry for me, put his arm around my shoulder and said, 'Don't worry, mate. I'll take it from here,' and walked me in. Which was really nice of him because in the scene I was meant to be the little brother who's a bit pissed off about him breaking up with my sister.

'I DON'T WANT TO BRAG, BUT I'M ON THIS TV SHOW'

Pete
So your first day was a bit shit, granted. What about when you first watched it back? What did you think?

A trendy club about fifteen years ago

Sam
Fuck me, I loved it. I went to straight out to Embargo's, mate.

Pete
What, giving it the big one? Thinking everyone would know who you were? And did they?

Sam
No, not really. I'd have to tell people. I'd be like, 'I don't want to brag, but I'm on this TV show.'

Pete
Fucking tragic, mate.

Sam
Well, I used to be worse. Before I was even on the show I used to say to girls, 'My sister's on *Made in Chelsea*,' just so that they'd talk to me.

Pete
I give up! How the fuck are we mates?

Sam
The coolest thing that ever happened in my life was when I was in Shagaluf. Not shagging, mind...

Pete
Shock!... So Wankaluf, then.

Sam
Crankaluf, actually. Had a cry and a wank.

Sorry Mum, if you're reading this

Pete
Which is a technique Sam still uses to this day. It's better than spit.

Sam
Anyway, I was walking down the Magaluf strip and someone – a girl, a *female* – came up to me and said, 'You're Louise Thompson's brother.' Bro, I *died*. I just went, 'Drink now? Should we go? I'll take you anywhere you want.'

Pete
Jesus, you're easily pleased, mate.

Sam
It was – honestly – such an amazing moment... That was the first time I'd ever been recognised. It was epic!

Pete
I can't believe you remember your first time. I don't, at all. So once you settled in, did you study the rest of the cast to see how they stayed relevant on the show – like showmances, arguments, going to the park with a full face of

slap? Did you ever think about doing any of that, just to kind of get yourself out there?

Sam
Absolutely. I've always thought I was best on the fly, without really thinking too much.

Pete
True, thinking's not your strong point.

Ain't that the fucking truth

Sam
The more I overthink, the worse I get, then I end up being a bit weird. Jamie Laing, Proudlock and Spencer were the stars of the show, in the middle of these big storylines, and I knew I was never going to be like them, because I wasn't good-looking or old enough. So I decided I'd be the joke.

Pete
Don't put yourself down. I mean, you were fucking awful to look at.

Sam
I was terrible. I looked like Gollum. I could never do what you do, Pete, like walk on, be the new eye candy and hook up with someone who was really beautiful. I never had that luxury. So my only way of existing was to crack a gag or get naked. So that's what I did.

Pete
Fuck me, what an existence.

I'LL ASK HER OUT, SHE'LL PROBABLY SAY YES AND THEN WE'LL KISS

Sam
And so I desperately grafted the girls. I asked out this towering goddess called Fran Newman-Young, who is about six foot tall. She was around five years older than me, in her mid-twenties. I knew I didn't have a chance ... Well, actually, that's a fucking lie. I thought I actually *did* stand a chance, which is the most tragic thing, because I thought *Made in Chelsea* wasn't all that real. I thought if the camera was pointed at you, everyone would just play along. So I was like, okay, I'll ask her out, she'll probably say yes and then we'll kiss.

Pete
Isn't this the story where you took her back to your sister's house and then got your sister to serve you dinner before you started playing the violin *at* Fran.

Sam
Trumpet, actually.

Pete
You played a fucking trumpet? Fuck me! And then after you did that, you just went, 'Kiss?'

Sam
No, I pulled out some mistletoe.

Pete
Oh, you pulled out some mistletoe? That's better.

Sam
Actually, mistletoe drawn on a piece of paper. We filmed

it in June, so nowhere near Christmas, but it was what the mistletoe *symbolised*.

Pete
Which was what? That you're a total twat?

Sam
I held it up and went, 'Shall we?' She looked at me, appalled, and said, 'I've only just arrived.' And I said, 'What's the problem?' to which she cock-blocked me and said, 'No.'

I've *never* come back down to reality so fast. But we *did* go on a second date. And I made her a mixtape.

Pete
Oh my fucking god. Let's just stop the book here.

Sam
It was ace, though. On the front cover of the CD was a naked photo of me with a pot over my tackle...

Pete
You mean an egg cup?

Sam
And on the back of the case I held a pan over my arsehole. I had all the bangers on there, including the song from *Titanic*. I don't know why I had that on there.

Pete
Were you trying to cry her into bed?

Sam
I have no idea. But I *really* thought that was going to work. But it didn't. Then after that, she was like, 'We're not doing this any more' and walked off. So that was my first foray

into TV. I remember it incredibly well. Mainly because to start with I rarely got to film that much!

Pete
I mean, judging by these stories, I can see why. I, on the other hand, became a series regular on *TOWIE* and then it went a bit crazy. Girls I'd previously dated came out of the woodwork and sold kiss-and-tell stories even before my episodes aired. I couldn't believe the reaction, and I was pissed off that my private life was in the press because my mum and nan would read it. But at the age I was also, what straight guy wouldn't love a bunch of birds making you out to be a great lover? So I took it on the chin, 'cos in my head I still didn't think this would lead to a career.

Sam
I never thought of it as a career either. All I wanted was to party and be a bit of a legend for five minutes. Obviously that didn't happen, but I thought I could have a laugh before getting a real job.

Pete
Which would have been ... ?

Sam
An estate agent.

Pete
An *estate agent*?

Sam
Yeah, I thought that was the route I was gonna take. I was twenty-one.

Pete
I was older than you and I'd already set up my own business, so I planned to just go back to doing that.

I WAS ONE OF THE DOLPHINS THEY WANTED TO GET AWAY FROM

Pete
I settled into *TOWIE* pretty easily. The girls seemed to like me, but the lads were a different matter. When I first started some of them were pissed off that the new guy was getting lots of airtime. It was clear they'd had their feathers ruffled and they started slagging me off at every opportunity.

Now, I ain't the type of fella to just lie back and let some fucker get away with slagging me off. So a month in, we were filming a dinner scene where these geezers were all spouting off all these crappy in-jokes, some of which were directed at me. It didn't take long for my blood to boil, and I said to them, 'What's your problem with me?' They were shocked that I'd confronted them, but I think that was when they realised this long-haired wanker wasn't going away any time soon.

The minute I pulled them up on it, they changed their tune. But I didn't do that for the telly. I wasn't gonna sit there while they were all bitching behind my back. You've got a problem with me? Tell me to my face. I don't give a fuck whether you're on TV or not.

Fuck this sob story!

Sam
No one spoke to me. No one cared. It's not that they didn't like me, just nobody acknowledged me. But I didn't let it get me down. I had a crafty plan. When it came to shooting those event days where a bunch of the cast all turn up for a party or something...

Pete

Hang on, did you do the thing you still do now, where you just enter a conversation?

Sam

Bingo! You see, I'd let the producers think that I knew all the cast members, when in reality I didn't know any of them. So when filming started, I'd just stand in the background and wait for the right moment, and then step into a group of guys talking and say, 'What are we talking about, lads?'

Pete

Fuck me! And what would they do?

Sam

I'm not joking, they would literally move to a different part of the room, like a school of fish. And I was one of the dolphins they wanted to get away from.

Pete

Well, I'd probably do the same, to be honest.

Sam

But it gets sadder. At lunchtime, everyone would go for lunch with their different groups. I had no one, so my sister used to let me join her and Rosie and Binky.

Pete

Sounds a bit school playground, doesn't it?

Sam

Massively. I used to go and sit there with my sister and her friends, not even speaking, just eating my lunch on my own because no one would talk to me. But things changed when

I started dating on the show. That's when both of us started to make our mark.

SEX, LIES AND HEARTBREAK: DATING ON TV

Romance on reality TV is never simple. We faced love, heartbreak and a lot of awkward moments, all served to millions of viewers.

Pete
Relationships are what keep viewers hooked on reality shows. It's all about who's shagging who, who's doing the dirty behind someone's back, and who's about to get a drink chucked in their face when they get found out.

Sam
Usually me, as it goes.

Pete
Unlike Sam, I had a bit of a reputation as a ladies' man, which I guess wasn't exactly a lie, so my first few months on the show were basically just me getting to know most of the female cast. Then a year in, I met Megan McKenna on a night out and started dating her. As she was fresh off *Ex on the Beach* and *Celebrity Big Brother*, the press lapped it up and splashed us across the papers, and the *TOWIE* producers fell over themselves to sign Megs up to the show.

I'm not gonna lie, the rest of the cast were not happy about it. I think they could see from the amount of press we were already getting that viewers would be tuning in to see what the fuss was about. And fuck me – they did.

PEOPLE CALLED US THE TERRIBLE TWO OF ESSEX

Pete
For the next two years, most of the storylines were focused on Megan and me, and we could see some of the cast getting more and more aggy about it. It didn't help that she was as gobby as I was. That meant we were slap bang in the middle of every fucking drama going. But we had each other's backs. People called us the terrible two of Essex. We got on well and had the same sense of humour, so always had a proper laugh together. On top of that, we had the paps on our backs, trying to get pictures. It was mad.

Now, some reality stars would sell their kidney for that kind of shit. As you'll know, some of them fake relationships just to stay relevant on the show and in the press.

But Megan and I weren't like that. We were real. We were proper into each other, and the attention we got from the press was mad. This was when everyone watched *TOWIE* and long before there were a million other reality shows on the telly, so whatever we did got written about. But it was hard on Megan and me because we were just trying to have a real relationship.

I BECAME PUBLIC ENEMY NUMBER ONE

Pete
It was around this time that the lines were beginning to blur between TV me and real me. But then – fuck me – what do I go and do? Classic Pete! I go and fuck things up by sexting a couple of girls behind Megan's back.

Sam
Oh Pete. What an idiot. Why would you *do* that?

Pete

Because back then I thought I was the big I am, that I was a proper geezer. But I was young and stupid, and looking back I ain't proud of myself.

Sam

So what did you do? Go on the old charm offensive and become Pete the Snake Charmer?

Pete

Sam, I was the snake! I tried my best to sort it out, but it wasn't easy! You see, the press found out and ran it. It was rough. My mum read it. Megan read it. The nation read it. There was no hiding. I became public enemy number one. I got death threats. People spat at me in the street. I received videos of dolls made to look like me being strung up and set on fire. Complete strangers would scream 'cunt' at me in public.

Sam

That's really dark.

Pete

And all the while, Megan and I were trying to work through it because what we had was a genuine relationship. But it's hard, trying to fix something when the entire country is telling your girlfriend to leave you.

With the story blowing up in the press, we kind of had to address it on the show. When we were filming in Marbella, Megan completely ripped me a new arsehole on the beach, screaming, 'If you want to be single, be single then!'

Sam

Every time I've happened to have seen it, my arsehole totally tightens.

Pete

Imagine what mine felt like! But I went along with it. Why? I have no fucking clue. I think I just wanted to sort my real-life shit out with Megs. That's how blurred the lines had become between real life and reality TV.

Sam

And none of it was for the cameras?

Pete

What do you think? Megs and I were always authentic. All of our scenes were real. So what viewers saw in that beach scene was 100 per cent real. Yes, it was on camera and on the telly, but it was 100 per cent real. Our reactions were genuine.

Sam

You can tell. You can see the veins popping out on her neck when she's tearing into you!

Pete

I desperately wanted to save our relationship. I didn't give a fuck about the cameras. We were in the moment. We shot for hours, and when the producers got what they wanted, they left us alone. That was probably the realest reality you can get.

Sam

Knowing you as I do now, I can't believe you actually did that.

Pete

I know – I can't believe it either, as I have never really taken this reality bollocks seriously. I guess I got caught up in my real life. But I learnt a lesson and now keep my private life private.

Sam
Not that it stops the papers writing about you.

Pete
Well, I dredge up this story now because I reckon that whole situation is the main reason why I ended up with this reputation for being a ladies' man. It's stuck, and it pisses me off. There's this non-stop fascination about who I'm seeing. And that's why I stopped sharing my real relationships and personal life on *TOWIE*. I'd give bits, but it wasn't the same. Megs and I eventually went our separate ways, but I'm glad to say we're still mates now. She's married and has a kid of her own, and I've moved on with you, Sam!

IF YOU ACT LIKE A TWAT, YOU GET MORE SCREEN TIME

Sam
It was a little different for me. I did the opposite, and actually leaned into the drama of the show to get noticed.

Pete
You surprise me!

Sam
When I first joined *Made in Chelsea*, I didn't really get much screen time.

Pete
Is that because you were an insipid streak of piss?

Sam
Yeah, in those days I wasn't the professional reality star I would later become. To start with, I'd only appear in one scene an episode, if I was lucky.

Pete
I guess they didn't wanna scare off any viewers.

Sam
Then I decided I wanted to do more. So I studied the way Spencer Matthews behaved.

Pete
Sounds fucking creepy.

Sam
How he was always at the centre of the drama. I knew I was never going to be in the same league, I just wasn't as good-looking or charismatic as him, but I still reckoned I stood a chance with the girls because we were on the telly. So I started asking ridiculous people on dates.

Pete
Classic Sam!

Sam
I wrote one girl a poem and she agreed to go for a drink with me.

Pete
A poem? Who was she? Jane fucking Austen?

Sam
I was over the moon. But it didn't take long to discover that she'd only gone out with me because she wanted to be filmed.

Pete
That makes total sense.

Sam

But regardless, I made the most of the opportunity. It was then that it hit me: if you act like a twat, you get more screen time, which means you stay more relevant within that world. So I started acting like a prize idiot.

Pete

That must have been hard!

Sam

But the funny thing is, I actually enjoyed playing the fool.

Pete

Well, at least you found something you were good at.

Sam

Same as when I was at school: I loved being the class clown. Even when people made fun of me, I didn't care. As long as people laughed. So, in the end, it wasn't just getting more screen time, it was more about doing what I love – entertaining people.

Pete

So when are you gonna start doing that for me, then?

Sam

I'm a bundle of fun, Pete. You know it. You can't get enough of me.

Pete

I've had more than enough of you for this chapter. So put us all out of our misery and finish your story!

Sam

Sadly, my larking about on the show didn't really go down

as well as I hoped and I got a lot of online hate. At first, that sucked, but I took it on the chin and thought, Screw it. It'll get better.

To this day, I don't understand the hate I received, because I was just trying to have fun, but I kept telling myself that viewers never really liked newbies anyway.

And then I found romance and everything changed.

3

Dating and Drama
=
Relevance

AT FIRST SHE BLANKED ME

Sam

The producers invited me out for the back end of *Made in Chelsea: New York*, which quite honestly was one of the best summers of my life. I went out there for three and a half weeks, got absolutely obliterated and spent a ridiculous amount of money I didn't have. I don't regret it one bit. I stayed at Jamie and Spencer's, though I was officially supposed to be bunking up with Francis Boulle.

I spent all my time with Jamie and Spencer. They led me astray a little bit, but I think I wanted to be led astray. I saw them as big brothers. They'd argue all the time and it was funny to watch. I knew Jamie a little from the show, but only properly got to know him in New York, where we realised we were really similar.

Pete

In what way? That you both wore yourselves out at boarding school, playing soggy biscuit?

Sam

It was in New York where I met Tiff. At first she blanked me, but when we got back to London we started dating. We were just kids, so it was a bit of a rollercoaster, serious one minute, not so serious the next. We'd bicker and row and split up and get back together again. All on TV!

I also tried to be a bit of a jack the lad and started flirting with girls just for the drama. Naturally this upset Tiff a bit. At one stage, after we had a row I got with a girl in a club but then got ratted out by a cast mate.

Pete

Good old reality TV cast mates! Dropping you in it for their own bit of screen time.

Sam

And it all kicked off. Tiff confronted me, and I did the cowardly thing of saying it wasn't true. Not once, but four times. I was in full panic mode.

Pete

Ah, the old 'Deny! Deny!' Classic.

Sam

Tiff could see right through me, so I just came clean.

Pete

Wow, that's a fucking move. She take it well?

Sam

Nah, she broke down in tears, which was tough to watch. I

was so shocked by her reaction that I kind of froze, which must have made me look like I didn't care. I just didn't know what to do. I was a stupid skinny kid with no life experience. And then I started to panic again, as I thought that when the scene finally aired I was gonna look like a robot because I wasn't crying or anything.

Pete
What the fuck?

Sam
I was worried that if I didn't cry, I'd look like a knob.

Pete
Mate, you still sound like a knob!

Sam
And she dumped me anyway.

Pete
Well, she had every reason to.

Sam
To cut a long story short, we were on and off for a long time and then we ended up going our separate ways after I did *Celebrity Big Brother*. Having a relationship on TV is hard. On a show like *Made in Chelsea*, it kind of changes everything. It makes you more prominent – suddenly people start having opinions about you, about the relationship, and your whole 'plotline' on the show.

Pete
Tell me about it. People just love to fucking comment.

Sam

That whole Tiff era really felt like the turning point. What we had was real for the most part. Yes, for a time our relationship was part of the *Made in Chelsea* drama and I was fully aware that our ups and downs in real life meant that we were sometimes front and centre of the show.

Pete

Which is what most cast members would want.

Sam

I started out thinking that having a TV relationship might help me stay relevant and raise my profile within the series, but then real life intervened and genuine romantic feelings took over. Of course, along the way I did stupid things, but whether that was me playing up to the cameras or simply because I was just immature, I can't quite decide. I guess I was just young and naïve, and learning about life on the job ... I very quickly realised that despite being on a show, this was real life, and people's feelings were being hurt, including mine.

HAVING A RELATIONSHIP IS BREAD AND BUTTER FOR A LOT OF REALITY STARS

Sam

The thing is, viewers of shows like *TOWIE* and *Made in Chelsea* love watching people get together, fall out and break up. And some of the cast are quick to cotton on to that, and to engineer relationships to get screen time.

Pete

And the more screen time you get, the more work you can find.

Sam

Right, so here's the thing: magazines, telly, big brands – they absolutely love a hot young couple. And honestly, fair play: get in a cute relationship, do some Insta posts, land a few juicy deals.

Pete

Get some veneers, or a gob job, as I like to call 'em.

Sam

Then they split, have a massive social media fight and boom – they're on to the next high-profile fling. It's like a well-oiled machine. Completely mad, but kind of genius.

Pete

Romantic, ain't it?

Sam

But I have to admit that sometimes you really do fall for people in these situations, especially when you're in your early twenties and stuck in a weird reality bubble. Things can rapidly develop in a way you don't expect. When I did *Celebrity Big Brother*, Amelia Lily and I really did start to form a proper bond, because we were so tight, and because she was such a lovely person. I think deep down we both knew we weren't each other's type, but we got on so well. And when you find yourself in an awkward environment like the *CBB* house, it's easy to forge a close bond with someone. Before you know it, everyone's saying, 'You two should just get together.' So you kind of do. I think that's why so many people end up in these so-called showmances, because the link between television and real feelings can be complex.

4

The Public React

Being the star of a successful reality show can be great, as opportunities come your way. And while fans of the show may take to you, you also have to deal with the harsh reactions of the general population!

Pete
I know I bang on about how much I despise this whole vacuous fucking reality world, but I did have a good time. There, I said it! Hanging out with the cast from *TOWIE*, for example – the ones I got on with – was great. And I was lucky enough to do some genuinely exciting stuff. Foreign trips, mad nights out, getting pissed at parties. But the one thing I always found hard to deal with? The reaction from the public.

Sam
Oh yeah, the viewers can be brutal. The public hated me to start with. Like, properly hated me. For the first few years on *Made in Chelsea*, it was all, 'Who's this annoying guy?' or 'Who's this one trying too hard to be funny?' I got death threats.

Pete
Absolutely outrageous.

Sam
And it wasn't even like I did anything that bad! I just had this gap tooth, wasn't conventionally good-looking, and I liked to think I was quite charismatic. But back then, that didn't fly. It's different now ...

Pete
Well, the teeth are.

Sam
... but at the time, if you didn't look like you'd just walked off a catwalk, no one wanted to know. Seriously, they saw me as a spare part. 'Get this guy off the show.' But the funny thing is, I didn't care. I was just buzzing to be there. I enjoyed being part of it. I was having the time of my life. So it all kind of bounced off me. Now? I'd be like, 'Oh my God, that really hurts.' But back then? I didn't give a fuck.

I STILL DON'T UNDERSTAND WHY PEOPLE THINK IT'S ALL RIGHT TO SAY SHIT TO STRANGERS ONLINE

Pete
When you're filming the show, you get so involved in what's going on around you that you never think about how you are going to look when the episode actually goes out. But come Sunday night, when *TOWIE* aired, it was a nightmare. You'd sit there, that fucking theme tune would start and then you'd wait for your phone to blow up. And then you'd doomscroll through your social media and it'd be full of 'wanker', 'fucking prick', 'hope you die'.

Sam
Wow, you had it easy!

Pete
It was mental. I'd read through all of it, start counting how many times I got called names or told to die. It became like a drinking game – I'd be absolutely off my tits by the first advert break.

I know a lot of it is what they call 'panto banter' – the viewers just get caught up in the drama of the show and slag off the villains they love to hate. But I still don't understand what kind of prize cunt thinks it's all right to say the kind of shit they dare to say to a stranger online.

Sam
I mean, I'd love someone to walk up to me and say to my face what they say about me online ... Oh, wait, they do.

Pete
Just listen to the pod, mate, I'm always calling you a dopey bellend.

Sam
But you say that with love.

Pete
Do I? Anyway, when it all kicked off, I was the new guy on *TOWIE*, so people didn't really know me that well. The general vibe was, Oh, he's a bit angry, but he's all right. But once the whole storyline with Megan took off, it went to another level. For the first month or two, I found it funny. Not funny ha-ha, but I didn't let it get to me. I just thought, You don't know me. I was more focused on sorting things with Megan in real life than worrying about what some sad keyboard wanker was saying.

I HAD THE LOWEST OPINION OF MYSELF I'D EVER HAD

Pete

After three months ... six months ... nine months ... a year of it – non-stop – it started to wear me down. You hear something enough times, you start to believe it. I had the lowest opinion of myself I'd ever had. It was just relentless. And listen, I've got thick skin. I can take being called a cunt now and again, and to be fair, looking back at some of the shit I did on *TOWIE*, I can understand why some people would say it. But when it gets personal? When it gets really dark? That's when I tap out. That's when I start thinking: these sick, twisted bastards need to be locked up. I've had people threaten to hurt my dogs. That boiled my fucking piss. I mean, come on. Call me whatever you want, fine. But don't you fucking dare go near my dogs. That crosses a line.

Sam

That's totally out of order. Some people can be such twats.

Pete

Some of the press can be a bunch of tossers, but they're nowhere near as bad as they were back then. They were absolutely savage.

We were in the public eye before what happened to Caroline Flack. And after that, things did calm down a bit. People thought twice before saying anything and told everyone to be kind. But before then? Certain areas of the press didn't give a fuck about you. You weren't a person to them, you were just a headline. They didn't care what effect it had on your life, or the people around you.

Whatever was written about me, my mum and my nan would read it. And no one wants their family reading that kind of shit about them. Ever.

Social media was – and still is – a fucking free-for-all cesspit. No rules. No consequences. Back then, there wasn't a proper system to report stuff. So I tried not to take it personally. I mean, it says more about those fuckers than it does about me. That's always been my attitude. But when the hate is constant, day after day, you start thinking everyone must think that about you. It gets in your head.

For a while, I didn't want to go out anywhere. I was always on edge. Always waiting for someone to shout something or spit at me or say something sly. I was permanently tense and felt like I was fit to burst!

THE MORE OF A TWAT I WAS, THE MORE WORK I GOT

Pete
I'm a pretty good geezer overall.

Sam
I think we can all agree on that.

Pete
Yeah, I'm pessimistic, sarky and I say fuck a bit too much, but underneath the tattoos and the tan, I've actually got a good heart.

Sam
The biggest, mate. Everyone knows that!

Pete
The press, though? They never seemed to see that. They just saw the character I played on the show and never once tried to look any deeper. So they decided I was a love rat. A lothario. A proper walking red flag. And to be honest, for

a while I gave up trying to correct them. I just leaned into the angry villain role they'd given me. And you know what? The more of a twat I was, the more work I got.

Sam
Everyone loves a TV villain, don't they? Look at Simon Cowell, or Nasty Nick off of *Big Brother*.

Pete
Who? But it's true. Viewers love the villain. You think they're mean bastards, but they're usually fucking fun to watch. I get it. Drama sells. But what does that say about us as people, eh?

Sam
That we all love drama.

Pete
After Megan and I broke up, the reputation of being a bad boy just stuck. And that's when I became a full-blown caricature of myself. That's why I ended up doing shows like *Celebs Go Dating*, not once, but four times. Because people wanted to see me in some sort of relationship situation. That's what people seemed to love watching me do.

But what that meant was, no relationship was real. It was all for show. People didn't want *me*, they wanted the TV me. The flirty ladies' man, bad boy routine. That's what they were buying. And it helped keep me out there.

Sam
Staying relevant.

Pete
And to be fair, that still is me. I am flirty. I've got that side. I can turn on the charm. But if I had a pound for every

person the press said I was dating, I wouldn't be sitting here writing a book, I'd be retired in the Maldives.

Sam
And me. Don't forget me.

Pete
What do you mean? I can't forget you, you're sitting right next to me.

Sam
I wanna come and live with you in the Maldives.

Pete
Anyway, I was mid-flow. When the press latches on to you and you go along with it, you do end up becoming a version of yourself that isn't really you any more. You become a character. A brand. A storyline. And eventually, you realise it is hard to go back.

MY MUM ENDS UP IN CONVERSATIONS ABOUT ME IN TESCO

Pete
My family have been brilliant, but being in the public eye isn't easy for them. Sometimes they're dragged into it, which is completely out of order. I'm the one on the telly, not them.

My dear old nan always said I'd end up doing something like this. Right from when I was a kid. I never believed her, of course. I'd be like, 'What the fuck are you on about, Nan?' I wasn't an actor, I wasn't into drama, I wasn't that kind of kid.

But when I did end up on *TOWIE*, she absolutely loved it. She'd watch every episode and then call me after, tell me off or that I needed to apologise to someone, or tell me I should hold my head high. And I'd just do what she said. Because you live and die by the sword, don't you?

My mum, bless her, she's very different to me. She's not a big personality. She doesn't love the spotlight. She's quiet, gentle, and just wants a normal life.

Sometimes she finds it uncomfortable to be in public with me. When she goes to Tesco [Or any other popular supermarket] and goes to pay for something they'll ask her if she's Pete Wicks's mum! She ends up in fifteen-minute conversations about what I'm *really* like. Most of the time, it's fine, the public are always polite and respectful to her, but I don't like it. I mean, *I* put myself in that position – I didn't want to put everyone else around me in it. And that's what I dislike. Whereas for you, Sam, your family were already kind of in that world.

Sam

Not that it made it any easier for me. People liked Lou. People didn't like me. They didn't even notice me.

Pete

Sorry, did you say something?

Back in those early days, as I started getting a name for myself, my family never let me forget who I was or get carried away with it. They reminded me that it could all stop at *any* moment. They weren't being mean, just realistic. I still believe that now. It could all stop tomorrow. Once upon a time I used to have a contingency plan if it all disappeared – not a game plan, a *contingency* plan. But all these years later, I don't have that any more. I'm so far into this now, I genuinely don't know what else I could do. I've lost that 'I'll just go back to what I did before' thing. That's gone.

5

Personal Appearances

When you're on reality TV, the quickest cash comes from late-night PAs. They're not as glam as they sound. From nightclubs to shopping centres, we have faced our fair share of pissed-up hecklers and handsy fans.

Pete
So, we'd landed TV shows that made us relevant to some degree. But that was just the first step. In spite of appearing on the telly every week, we weren't exactly rolling in it. Truth is, you get around fifty quid a day for filming on those shows. That's all! It's not like a proper job where you get paid by the hour. You get paid with whatever loose change they've found down the back of the couch at the Sugar Hut!

Sam
So, what most of us do to supplement our income is get work outside of the show, like mag deals and brand sponsorships.

Pete
But one of the best ways of making good dosh is doing PAs.

I did so many of the bastards that I was nicknamed PA Pete. Or Pirate Pete, thanks to the long hair and tatts.

Sam
On paper, doing a PA sounds like a piece of piss. But let me assure you, it's not.

Pete
It's fucking hard work. Not just because you have to travel all around the country through the night after a hard day's work, but also 'cos you have to deal with a bunch of pissheads who think they're funny.

Sam
First of all, let me explain what usually happens at a PA. You arrive at the venue, get announced on stage, maybe get up in the DJ booth, answer a few questions from the audience and then do a meet and greet and have some pics taken.

Pete
Bear in mind these events usually happen around one in the morning, so the kind of questions you'll get asked by this crowd are nothing as eloquent as 'So, tell us how you got into TV.' Instead, some lairy twat will ask, 'Would you shag me mum?'

Sam
People who turn up to these nights have clearly left their inhibitions at home. To be fair, most of them have probably been knocking back pints of cheap lager and blue WKD since they got out of work or college, so you can't really blame them for being in the sorry state they are in. I'm sure we were just the same at their age.

Pete

Only difference being, I wouldn't be at some shit club to see some no-talent reality star!

Sam

Now, as Pete has said, he was the king of the PA circuit. I, on the other hand, was not. In fact, in the early days of *MiC* I was rarely booked for any and would just tag along with Jamie Laing and Alex Mytton. And I loved it.

Pete

There really is no end to how desperate you are.

Sam

Mate, I would literally *pay* to get into clubs and hang out with them. I would just be there. Lurking.

Pete

That's when having the rep of being a serial ladies' man from the country's most talked about reality show comes in handy. Club promoters book you because they know you're gonna bring the punters in. No offence, Sam ... but who's gonna fall over themselves to touch up the geek from *Made in Chelsea* in some hot and sweaty piss-soaked club in the back of beyond?

Sam

Tell me about it. One of the first of a very few paid PAs I did was in a club up north. I'd driven there all by myself. Super excited. But that didn't last long. When I was announced on stage I was met by a tsunami of boos. Like, thunderous, loud booing. I didn't know what to think. But then it got worse.

Pete
How? They thought you were Gollum?

Sam
Someone chucked a kebab at me.

Pete
Classy joint!

Sam
Luckily I ducked in time, so it didn't hit me. And then the DJ begged the crowd to stop being mean to me! It was horrible and I felt bad because I didn't understand why they were being so horrid.

Pete
Because they're pied up and lairy. And they were probably expecting one of the sexy Chelsea girls. Or Pirate Pete!

Sam
Once I got off stage, I bought a massive round of Jägerbombs.

Pete
You did what??!?

Sam
I bought people in a certain section of the bar a drink.

Pete
Why the fuck did you do that?

Sam
Because I just wanted people to like me.

Pete
Oh Sam, mate, you can be a tool sometimes. Thank God you've got Uncle Pete to help stop this sort of shit happening.

Sam
Grandpa Pete, more like.

Pete
Don't push it, or I'll throw a kebab at you!

Sam
It was such a shame, because all the PAs I had gone to with Alex and Jamie had been so fun. Everyone had been friendly, even when I wasn't supposed to be there. But when I was actually booked for a PA by myself or alongside other cast mates, it was awful, as no one would stand in my queue. They'd all line up for the others instead and I'd be like, 'Hey!' But they'd still ignore me or, even worse, ask me to take a picture of them with Jamie or Alex! You see, I was never the cheese, always the hanger-on.

Pete
I'm actually starting to feel sorry for you, mate, you poor, sad sap!

Sam
Looking back, I think I struggled doing PAs 'cos I'm basically a massive people-pleaser, and I'd want to talk to *everyone*, take photos, hug people. I didn't have security or anything. I just wanted everyone to have a good time. But it was exhausting, pouring out all that energy, so I found it very hard to deal with.

Pete
That's why I always say get in, do the job, take some pics and fuck off home. I mean, I've seen it all. At one gig, a girl was waiting so long in the queue to see me that she pissed herself when she hugged me.

Sam
Could have been worse. Could have shat on you!

Pete
At a Pirate Party on the Isle of Man, three generations of a family came out to see me, including their old nan who hadn't been out of the house for about fifteen years and arrived on a fucking Zimmer frame with a parrot on her shoulder.

Sam
A parrot? A *real* parrot?

Pete
What do you think? I've had couples have a barney right in front of me because the boyfriend would get fed up of having to take a million pictures of his girlfriend climbing all over me like a kids' climbing frame.

Sam
Quite rightly so!

Pete
When I was promoting my best-selling calendar, I did a PA in a shopping mall in Derby where this poor girl waited ages in the queue only to faint right in front of me.

Sam
Oh my God, was she all right?

Pete

She was fine in the end, but it shocked the fucking life out of me.

Sam

Talking about pissing and passing out, remember that time we did that PA in Dundee?

Pete

Barely. I tend to put most of these nightmare stories out of my mind as fast as I can.

Sam

This was during the early days, and we were so excited to have been invited to this club that we said yes without asking any questions. Turns out we were last-minute replacements for Tommy Fury and that the two of us would be sharing his fee.

Pete

That certainly never happened again!

Sam

It was a nightmare. When we got out on stage everyone was chanting 'Where the fuck is Tommy? Where the fuck is Tommy?' We just stood there awkwardly. Anyway, cutting to the best part of this story . . .

Pete

Oh, there is a point to this trip down memory lane, then?

Sam

I must've eaten something bad that night because on the way home I was throwing up *and* shitting my arse out at the back of an easyJet flight.

Pete
Oh yes ... I'm starting to remember it.

Sam
I was literally lying face down in Pete's lap.

Pete
Which from a distance looked pretty fucking weird.

Sam
It was awful. But as soon as we landed it got worse. Our driver saw the state I was in and was like, 'Right, I'm off!' and drove off in his Jag, leaving me literally shitting behind a bush with one hand outstretched, begging him 'Don't leave me!' Then all of a sudden a car pulls up behind me and someone goes, 'Oh my God – is that Sam Thompson shitting in a bush?' And as I don't like to let anyone down, I looked up, flashed them a big Sam smile and gave them a 'Hello'.

Pete
And the point of all this?

Sam
You know what? I don't know. I think I just wanted to explain that doing PAs wasn't always a lark. They could also be messy!

Pete
Point well made. Next?

IF SOMEONE WENT TOO FAR, I'D GIVE MY TOUR MANAGER A LITTLE SIGNAL

Pete

While doing PAs was a bit of a laugh to start with, I eventually had enough of people touching me, picking me up or manhandling me in general and calling me every name under the sun. So I hired a tour manager. I kind of had to, after I'd had a bit of a nasty face-off with some cheeky geezer.

I told this fella, 'Say what you want to me, but don't take the piss. I'm still just a normal bloke.' That's when I realised I needed someone to make sure we avoided getting into any trouble. So me and my tour manager came up with a little code. If someone went too far I'd give him a signal, and he'd get them out of there. It worked most of the time. And trouble was avoided.

What I Hate About Modern Life, by Pete Wicks

Pete
I know I am a miserable old bastard most of the time, but I can't help it. I like what I like, and I like who I like. But as I hurtle towards death – which really can't be too far away these days – I can't help but get angry. There are so many things that piss me off. That get on my wick. But what mainly pisses me off is people. People as a whole. I just struggle with them. I really do. I think they cause so many problems in the world. Or just irritate me. Don't get me started on those people who play music out loud on their phone. I mean, what is that about? Put some fucking earphones on, you tit. I don't want to hear your tuneless crap!

If I could, I would run away and live on my own island with dogs. And then I would invite the people that I tolerate now and then for short periods – not for a long period – so I still have that human connection.

But technology is probably the biggest thing at the minute for me. AI and that – it's giving people that lack personality a sort of personality. But it's just the same personality as everyone else. AI is far more intelligent than most people I know. And actually has more feelings than most people I know, which is mad, because that's the one thing AI doesn't possess.

Sam
What's mad is that I couldn't think more opposite. I love people. I love a hug. I just adore that.

Pete
There is no need for human touch.

Sam
I'd say that everyone needs to have at least a five-second hug a day. Latching onto somebody like a tick.

Pete
See, the way you just said that, the way you're describing it, makes you sound like a pest.

Sam
I love that about life. Just latching onto a person, giving them a big old squeeze, staying there for a little bit too long. People are great, because everybody has an energy that can transfer from one person to another. And AI is great as well, because you can have a relationship with AI now. Genuinely – and I mean this, Pete – if I don't have a girlfriend, I'm gonna go out with AI and I have no problem with that. At all.

Pete
Is that a healthy thing to do? Of course it's not. You can't do anything physical with it.

Sam
Well, I can pleasure myself and make it watch.

Pete
Okay, moving on! One of my least favourite things in the world is forced fun. So, for example, when I got dragged along to see those Jellycats being 'cooked' at that café in Selfridges, it was my fucking idea of hell. I just don't understand it.

Listen, everyone likes different things, and everyone's entitled to that. But you can't convince someone to like what you like just because you like it. And I think that's what a lot of people do. 'It's because you don't understand!' No,

I do understand Jellycats. I understand the concept. You don't need to explain it to me. But it's fucking ridiculous. Me going there is not gonna make me go, 'Oh, I get it now. I get it.' I thought it was stupid that they 'cook' toys before I went, now that I've seen it I still think it's stupid. I was right. You're not going to change my mind because now I 'get it'. Don't give me some bollocks like 'it's food for the soul'.

Sam
That's exactly what it is. It's food for the soul.

Pete
It's not food. It's not food. It's not food.

Sam
It puts smiles on faces. It's also more for older people. We love it.

Pete
It's not for older people.

Sam
It is.

Pete
No, it's for children. And I get it, for children. It's great. If your kid wants to go and be delusional and think that they're frying fish and chips, then that's fine. But if you're an adult, you should know better. Do better. Go and read books. Go and do something that's normal. Don't go and fry a toy, you fucking cretin.

Sam
I would say that I think that it obviously moves people in a way that, you know, other things don't?

Pete
Sam's lying. The reason he enjoyed it is because I hated it.

That's why Sam enjoyed it. Sam went and enjoyed it so much because he saw how uncomfortable it was for me and how much I hated it. Sam wouldn't go to the Jellycat thing on his own. If Sam went out on a Saturday night on his day off, he'd go for dinner in a nice restaurant. He'd have a drink. What he wouldn't do is go to the Jellycat Café.

Sam
I like the idea of it.

Pete
You like the idea that I don't like the idea.

Sam
I would go with Producer Pippa.

Pete
You just go with Pippa. Why did you have to drag me?

Sam
Because it's more fun with you.

Pete
No, because the only reason that you found it fun was because I didn't.

Sam
It *is* very fun when Pete doesn't like things.

Part 2

Almost Relevant

6

Next Steps

There's only so much time you can live your life on reality TV. So what next? Well, when you're clueless about the telly world, you need some help to stay relevant enough to get more work. Enter the manager!

Pete

About six or seven months into *TOWIE*, juggling all the PA invites was starting to get a bit much and I felt like I needed to try something else. I wanted to find new challenges, I needed help – proper help. A manager, like some of the other cast members had, who could take the reins and sort the hard stuff out for me. And – unbeknownst to me – this would ultimately lead to meeting Sam. I was looking for someone who could guide me through the industry, deal with people, make contacts for me, get me other jobs

This is where Staying Relevant was written in the stars

Thing was, I didn't know what I wanted to do, or actually *could* do. I had no real talent – I mean, I wasn't a singer or an actor or a musician. The only thing I seemed to be good at was being a bit of a charmer. For me, *TOWIE* was always supposed to be a temporary gig. I never expected to stay in it for almost a decade. But doors were starting to open. The press were writing about me and people were showing interest, but I didn't really know what the plan was. I had to figure something out. I was introduced to a few managers, but they all seemed to be talking bullshit, saying, 'We'll get you to Hollywood! We'll make you a star!' I just sat there thinking, What are you on about? I can't act, how the fuck is that supposed to happen? It all sounded so fucking ridiculous.

Then I met Vicky Pattison at a PA and we clicked straight away. She suggested I speak to her management, Mokkingbird. Her team had recently left a bigger agency and started one of their own, and had taken on Vicky as their first client and become hugely successful. Gemma and Nadia, who run the team, were lovely – properly down to earth.

When I went to meet them, they sat me down and asked, 'What do you want to do?' I was honest and said, 'I don't know.' They explained that they wanted to work with talent who had a long-term game. Well, fame wasn't what I was after, but I was interested in making the most of what was on offer. They told me they saw potential in me – whatever that was – and that together we could work on a plan that was beneficial for both of us. I liked what they said to me. They were being real, none of that 'we'll take you to Hollywood' bollocks.

And so I signed with them and have never looked back.

For a long time, I never really had an end goal. When I was working in recruitment, I knew what path I was going to take. But in this world, I didn't have a Scooby about where I could go with it. It wasn't something I had ever considered for myself.

It's only in the last couple of years – since *Staying Relevant* took off – that things have started to feel more focused for me. Now Sam and I have set up a production company, hired an amazing team, got our own studio and have been developing lots of projects. I finally feel like I have something that feels solid to look forward to.

Sam
We're building something properly now and we want to grow it, bring other people in and see where it can go. It's so exciting. We've taken control and are doing our own thing. It's like a proper business.

Pete
It *is* a proper business. And why do we do it? Well, aside from earning a living I also have this weird sense of responsibility, like maybe we can bring a bit of light to what is, quite frankly, a fucking shit world. And I actually want to do that.

Same goes for writing this book. Of course we're getting paid – you fuckers bought it, cheers for that. But I'm hoping that somewhere in here, you'll smile.

Sam
And maybe even cry!

Pete
And if that happens, then it's fucking worthwhile. It's those little moments, when you can make someone laugh, or feel something, that's a nice fucking feeling. I don't know how or why we're able to do that, but I like it.

WE OWE A LOT TO OUR TV SHOWS – THEY GAVE US A PLATFORM AND THE CHANCE TO DO THINGS WE NEVER EXPECTED

Pete
Once I got myself a manager, the offers started coming in. Different shows, random opportunities ... and I just kind

of got swept up in it all. I didn't really know what I was doing – I'm glad someone did, and I just went with it. And together we managed to achieve so much.

Not only did I land appearances on more shows, I also got the chance to do things that actually made sense to me. I was already doing a bit of charity work – especially with dogs – but it was never something I talked openly about. I started working with a dog charity and took part in events for various other good causes. That was the first time I felt like I was doing something worthwhile in this whole world. I wasn't just going to nightclubs and being a dick. I had the chance to do some good with the platform I'd been given.

I think that was always the issue for me – feeling like none of it really mattered. Like it was all a big joke. I still don't know if it's a world I want to stay in. But more opportunities to do cool stuff just kept coming. I owe a lot to *TOWIE*, as does Sam with *MiC*. They have given us a platform and the chance to do things we never expected – I've fought off a shark on Bear Grylls's show, danced like a twat on *Strictly Come Dancing*, headlined the O2 with Sam for our very own podcast, had a *Sunday Times* best-selling book, presented my own award-winning TV show, *For Dogs' Sake*, presented a radio show with my mate Olivia Attwood, launched a mental health podcast called *Man Made* and have become ambassador for some amazing charities. I've done things I never thought I'd do, like stripping off on stage for charity on *The Real Full Monty* for ITV, or climbing mountains to help raise funds for Coppafeel. All incredible things. Now that I've written that down, I must admit I'm pretty chuffed. Who'd have thought a fucker like me could have done so much! But let's not get too carried away ...

Sam

It's been a total pleasure to be able to help raise awareness and money for charities like UNICEF and ADHD UK, and make some kind of difference. It makes all the showbizzy stuff we get to do seem justified. It's our chance to give something back for all the opportunities we have been given by people who offered us work and the public who have supported us along the way.

EVERYONE FEELS ENTITLED TO A BIT OF YOU – BUT YOU CAN'T BE A DICK ABOUT IT

Pete

It was the team at Mokkingbird who really made me think seriously about all this. I realised that maybe I had something different to offer. I don't want to sound up my own arse, but because I've always said what I like and been unapologetically myself in everything I've done, I never faded into the background on shows. So when producers see that you make good TV, more opportunities tend to come your way. It wasn't a calculated thing, I wasn't performing, it was just who I was. I'm not shy. I'm confident in all sorts of situations, so naturally I stood out. And that's what they want – someone who brings energy, who makes things happen on screen.

But the hard part is that you've got to be on your A-game constantly. Even just walking down the street. People come up wanting pictures, and if you're hanging out your arse and just want to be left alone, it's tough. Someone asks for a photo and in your head you're thinking, I can't be arsed, but you can't say that. That's not fair. It's like everyone feels entitled to a bit of you. And the truth is, you can't be a dick about it. Even though, to be fair, a lot of people in this industry manage it quite easily.

I WENT FOR TV SHOWS, INTERVIEWING JOBS BUT NO ONE WANTED ME

Sam

My story is not quite as fruitful as Pete's. I'd been on *Made in Chelsea* for about two years and was thinking about what I could do next. Like Pete, I could see these doors opening – broadcast, radio, presenting, interviewing people, different TV shows – and I thought, Oh my God, I want to do all of those things. But I found it hard. The truth is, back in the early days of reality, and being on a show like *MiC*, it was actually harder to get through those doors unless you were a real stand-out character.

The only reason I even knew those doors existed was because of reality TV. But the twist was that being in reality TV meant I couldn't go through them, because people like me weren't considered cool enough by producers of certain shows. It was a complete double-edged sword.

I tried desperately to break into radio for years, but no one wanted me. I was told I was the wrong demographic. Too posh. And to be fair, I kind of get that. I went for jobs as an interviewer, but nothing. Tried for sports presenting – same story. TV shows – no one wanted me.

At one point I was so frustrated that I asked one of the top bods on *Made in Chelsea* about getting an agent. She just looked at me and said, 'You're not there yet.' Brutal. So I asked, 'Okay, well, what do I need to do?' And she kind of shrugged and went, 'There's no point.'

But I didn't give up. I kept pushing. I said, 'Can you at least set up a meeting with someone?' And eventually, she did. I got a meeting with an agent – again, someone connected to *MiC* – and was told the same thing: 'It's not the right time. You're nowhere near that.' So yeah, I got double-dipped.

Eventually, I did get an agent, but over the course of two

years I only got a couple of brand deals. For a time I felt like I was the lowest of the low. Literal pond scum. Right at the bottom of the food chain for two solid years. But eventually things did change. I clawed my way up. There was nothing else I wanted to do, so I just ... stuck it out, met my best friend and ended up where I am now.

7

Money is Relevant

Bored of messy PAs, we quickly learned there's money to be made in other ways...

Pete
So we'd made a few bob from PAs, but the novelty of getting paid to get pissed at a club soon started to wear thin. In order to become sort of relevant in the industry and be taken a bit more seriously, we had to find other things to do with what few skills we had. In the early days, we couldn't afford to be choosy and would find ourselves agreeing to do the maddest of jobs. Like turning up to the opening of a kebab shop for a couple of hundred quid.

Sam
No way!

Pete
Yeah, I cut a ribbon and everything.

Sam
I would've loved a kebab shop opening. Loved it.

Pete

Mate. Nothing says 'What am I doing with my life?' like being twenty-five and cutting the ribbon at Dave's Doner.

Sam

That would have been the dream. Back then, social media wasn't like it is now. There were no influencers and not many brand deals flying about. Especially for fellas, it just wasn't a thing. And if it was, it was like £200 to wear some bedroom-brand T-shirt. As fashion brands tend to focus on the girls, guys have a limited window. If it's not PAs, it's calendars, where you've got to pout and smoulder and give off this 'come to bed, I'm gonna shag you' look. Sweet!

Pete

During my first year on *TOWIE*, some bright spark suggested that I release a calendar. I was like, 'Why? No one's gonna buy that.' But fuck me! It outsold Justin Bieber in the UK. I mean, come on, who the fuck wants a half-naked me looking like a fucking Twiglet in a wig hanging on their fridge? Do something better with your money. What's wrong with you?

I did another calendar the year after, shot in Ibiza. I had a great time, did the photos, got absolutely hammered. Perfect. Did it again the year after that... no one bought it.

And that's when I was reminded yet again that this shit might not last for ever. But I didn't get upset about it. I just thought, All right, that was fun. What's next? That's how I looked at it for a long time.

Sam

Yeah, things started to change when *Love Island* became massive. We'd go to events and people didn't care about us. We felt like yesterday's news – it was all about the *Love Island* lot. And rightfully so, 'cos the show was massive. The public loved it. *I* loved it! Suddenly all these jobs we'd be getting started going their way, because they were younger, better-looking, fresher than us. They saturated the whole scene.

Pete

You'd see them doing these massive deals – like Ovie Soko, who did *Love Island* and is also looked after by my management, the only other guy they've got on their roster. He was out there working with Hugo Boss and Christian Louboutin, and being considered for campaigns with Gigi Hadid in New York. And I'm like, 'So ... we got any work?'

'Yeah, yeah, John West tuna want you to do—'

'Sorry, what?'

But you'd still do it. Because, as the old saying goes, make hay while the sun shines. That's where the money comes in. Over the years, we've done so many of them. And the brands have got better, like Burger King, Coors, Lynx, Vodafone, Phillips ... Don't get me wrong, if John West came calling again, I'd be more than happy to dress up as a fisherman – for the right price, of course!

Sam

And I did a campaign for Subway in collaboration with ITV. We have definitely come a long way!

Pete

For people like us, who aren't actors or musicians but podcasters and – let's be honest – fucking talentless no-marks, sponsorship deals are part of the job. Without them, we wouldn't make a penny.

Sam

Sponsorships make us money. When we advertise something on the pod, it's because we're a brand now, that's how we earn. People complain, like, 'Oh, the ads are annoying,' and I get it. But without them, there'd be no podcast.

8

Building Your Brand

Okay, so we'd made a name for ourselves, and now it was time to do something different. But what could we do next? How could do we maintain the level of fame we'd achieved and how could we grow and become a brand, which is so important when you're trying to stay relevant.

God, we sound like media wankers, don't we?

I WORE MY SISTER'S DRESS AND GOT FIFTY THOUSAND INSTA LIKES!

Sam

When I first started out on *Made in Chelsea,* Twitter was the platform everyone was using. Celebs posted their feelings on it, commented on press inaccuracies and even got into blazing rows. They would also be deluged with comments from the public, most of which were nasty! Then towards the end of my time on the show, Instagram was starting to become a thing and so I jumped on it and started making silly little videos, just for fun, way before anyone was doing branded content. I thought it was an exciting new platform, 'cos I could be creative and funny.

One of the first things I did was spoof *Celebrity Big Brother,* way before I ever went on it. I did a sketch where

I pretended to be a washed-up celeb who'd had a couple of reality TV relationships and who gets a big offer: is it the jungle? Nope... it's Big Brother! I still have that video. I was twenty-three, just messing about.

But the real turning point was when I started wearing my sister's clothes. That was it. That was the moment.

Pete
You kinky bastard! I bet you got off on wearing all her gear.

Sam
Maybe I did. Jokes! Nah, it was all for the 'gram! Every Sunday I'd post a photo wearing one of her outfits.

Pete
But why? Did we all need to see you with your arse hanging out of one of her bikinis?

Sam
Well, you see, Lou was one of the first people doing brand deals on Instagram. She'd post pictures dressed up in outfits from a brand, all polished, captioned with #ad. She was trying so hard. I thought, You know what? I'm gonna take the piss. I put on the exact same outfit she'd worn, did the same pose, same everything, and posted it. It blew up. I remember exactly how many likes it got: fifty thousand. Which was insane, considering no one knew who I was. I got loads of comments – even from famous people. Lydia Bright commented, and I just thought, This is nuts. They know about me, bruv!

Pete
Yeah, I remember being on *TOWIE*, seeing all this, and saying to the cast, 'What a fucking helmet. What a loser.'

Sam

And now I'm up your arse.

Pete

And getting dicked by you dressed as Spider-Man.

Sam

Yeah. You've come down to my level. But that was the moment I realised that just being fun on Instagram could actually work. Because honestly, not many people were doing it. Do you remember how seriously people used to take themselves on there?

Pete

I used to do a bit of sponsorship stuff. Brands would go, 'Here's a T-shirt. Post a nice photo in it.' That was it.

Sam

Or you'd hold a bottle of shampoo and strike a pose.

Pete

I used to get loads of hair stuff 'cos of my lanky pirate barnet. I'd post a pic with my hair done, holding the bottle, and say, 'I use this every day.' That would be the caption. Then this idiot started making all these weird, funny videos that weren't ads.

Sam

Yeah, but that was just it – not many people were doing it! And you know what's wild? It was way before I was getting paid for anything. I just did it because, one, it resonated with people, and two, I actually enjoyed making them. I got to be myself, be silly, and it actually worked.

When my sister started dating Ryan Libbey, her baby daddy and all-round lovely guy, they used to go on holiday and post these cringey workout videos.

Pete

Like what? Him lifting her up in the air doing bicep curls and all that?

Sam

Spot on! So I started to parody what they did with Tiff, when we were together. We pretended to be them, mimicking their every move. And again, it went off. I had so many likes and comments. I realised that I'd found my niche, so decided to double down on the videos. However, even with all that public interest, no one in the TV industry appeared to notice. Or care. And that's when it dawned on me that it can be such a cliquey space and that there are so many hoops you've got to jump through – just to get in the room, where no one wants to take a risk on anyone new.

IF YOU'RE NOT SEEN ON THE TELLY, THE OFFERS START TO DRY UP

Sam

As we started to find our feet and understand that there was a bigger world out there for us to explore, we had to make some tough decisions.

Pete

I finally quit *TOWIE* in 2022, after almost ten years. By then, my career was going well. Work was coming in and of course we had started *Staying Relevant*. As much as I moan about it, the show had been good to me. By that point I'd built up a good reputation, made a few bob, but I'd got to the point where I just wasn't enjoying it any more. There were loads of new cast members and I was getting bored of being the feisty one.

I knew I couldn't go back to the old career. I mean, who in their right mind would take me seriously? I realised it would be harder to find extra work if I wasn't seen on the telly. That's how you get forgotten – you are no longer seen as relevant, and then the offers of extra work start to dry up.

How many people have been on *Love Island* or *Celebs Go Dating* and suddenly just disappeared?

Looking back, I think I stayed longer on *TOWIE* than I should have, just to keep the work coming in elsewhere. That was the trade-off for me – doing other shows off the back of it. To help build some kind of brand for myself.

I was lucky. Because my profile had gone through the roof on *TOWIE*, and the viewers now seemed to like me, I was getting offered a fair amount of TV work.

I did stuff like *Celebrity Island, Pointless, Celebs Go Dating*. I came third on *The Weakest Link* – I was the strongest link the whole way through but they still booted me out. Probably because I was taking the piss and calling Laurence Llewelyn-Bowen 'Dad' the whole time. I won *Tipping Point* and did *The Hit List* with my mates Marvin and Rochelle Humes. I pretty much did every show out there. Sometimes more than once, but I won't bore you with a list – just google it and try to work out which shows I haven't done.

I HAD A TOTAL BREAKDOWN AND GAVE A PIG A SEA BURIAL

Pete

One of the first major shows that took me in a different direction was Channel 4's *The Island*. It was a proper survival show that saw a bunch of celebs being dumped on an island to see how they'd cope without all the mod cons they're used to in the real world. So, no mobiles. No tech. Nothing. It was also the kind of show that didn't feature many reality stars, so I was chuffed to be asked. I'm guessing I was chosen because someone dropped out at the last minute and some desperate producer got straight on the blower and went 'get that moany one off *TOWIE* who looks like a pirate!' But who cares? I was just excited to join up. Not because it was another TV show, but because of the experience I'd have. A month on a desert island? How could I turn that down? And I loved it. But fuck me, it wasn't easy!

I might look like a bit of a geezer, but when I was out there, I had a total breakdown. I should have known what to expect. I mean, you're there to survive. I made friends with a pig that everyone wanted to eat. I spent most of my time protecting it. And then what does it go and do? It goes and gets itself killed. I cried like I'd lost a family member. I had to beg the rest of the camp not to eat it out of respect for me. And even though some of them grumbled about it, they let me give it a sea burial and watched me swim the poor little fucker out into the sea in the pouring rain.

There were some legit stars on that show. I mean, you had Hollywood actor Eric Roberts – brother of Julia – who'd been in loads of films, including *The Dark Knight* with Heath Ledger. Then there was Jo Wood, Ronnie Wood's ex-wife, telling stories around the campfire about being on tour with the Rolling Stones. Martin Kemp chatting about being mates with George Michael and Freddie Mercury. Anthony Ogogo and James Cracknell sharing stories about their sporting successes. And me? I had nothing to say apart from, 'I like Greggs.' And I'm sat there thinking, What the fuck am I doing here? It was one of those proper out-of-body moments. Like, What is my life now?

For a long time, I genuinely thought all the proper celebs were judging me – like I didn't belong there, like I wasn't worthy. And to be fair, I still get that feeling when I'm around people I consider actually famous. I always feel a bit out of place, like I've snuck in through the back door.

But as it turned out, I ended up getting close with James Cracknell. He was going through a rough patch and we bonded, which surprised the hell out of both of us. Before the show, I was convinced we were gonna hate each other. He told me afterwards that he thought the same – 'Here we go, another fucking reality kid.' But the minute we met we just clicked, because we were like the camp workhorses. Up early every morning, sorting things for everyone else. That kind of became our thing. I took charge, because that's just who I am. Didn't matter who else was there. I was like, 'Right, James, you go do this.' He's a double Olympic gold medallist or something – and I'm sending him off to get water.

We had an odd friendship, but he's a top bloke. Dry sense of humour. He's genuinely a decent fella with a mad work ethic. Didn't have anything to prove. Me? I felt like I had everything to prove. I was surrounded by all these amazing, accomplished people . . . and then there was me, some useless prick off a reality show.

In the end, I think James and I bonded because I was only ever being me. That's all I know how to do. Whether I'm with celebrities or normal people, it's the same. I'm just going to do it my way. Always have.

Being part of that show was the first time I properly thought, This is actually quite cool, and that it could be a career. It was a mad show, a proper life experience and something I'll carry with me till the day I die. Up until that point, I'd just been drifting – falling into things and not really thinking about it. Now I knew what I wanted to do.

9

Building Your Brand Part 2

EVERYONE TOLD ME *CELEBRITY BIG BROTHER* WOULD RUIN MY CAREER. WHAT CAREER?

Sam

Doing all that social media stuff was what really raised my profile and set me apart from everyone else. It was Instagram that got me noticed by producers on some of the smaller TV shows. They saw me having a laugh, taking the piss, building a following. That's part of the reason I landed *Celebrity Big Brother*, which was massive for me.

It was the first big show I did outside of *Made in Chelsea*, and was when I started to feel like my own person. I remember thinking, I'm going to do *Big Brother*. Everyone around me was saying, 'Don't do it. It'll ruin your career.' But I said, 'I don't have one!' I wanted a chance to show the world the real me. God, that sounds cheesy. But I hoped people watching it would see more of me than they had on *Made in Chelsea*, where I was one of so many characters and mildly irritating.

thought you said very annoying

I was also stoked to do it as I'd watched *Big Brother* as a kid and had always dreamed about sitting in that legendary chair and saying, 'Oh my God, I'm on *Big Brother*.'

The cast was great. Sarah Harding from Girls Aloud, TV psychic Derek Acorah, Paul Danan – who have sadly all passed. Funnywoman Helen Lederer, Shaun Williamson (Barry from *EastEnders*), a Real Housewife and UK reality stars like Jemma Lucy, Jordan Davies from *Ibiza Weekender* and Amelia Lily from *The X Factor*! I had a great time. It was exhausting. But I learnt a lot.

Surprisingly, I got on well with Jordan. When he bounced through those doors I was worried we wouldn't get along as I'm so awkward and he was an ultra-lad, but I was proved totally wrong and he surprised me. Whether it was his ridiculous, almost superhuman energy levels that made mine look like a half-flat battery, or just the way he brought positivity into every room.

I'd have dips, I'd have moments where I was flagging, wondering what I was doing, whether I was being annoying – but he never did. He was always on. Always up. And not in a fake way either. It was just who he was. He lifted the whole house. Including me. Same story with Jemma. I ended up absolutely loving her. She was straight-up, no-nonsense. She treated everyone, especially the older housemates, with genuine respect. She helped out in the kitchen, cleaned up, didn't act like she was above anything. She's a proper grounded, compassionate woman.

And then there was Shaun Williamson – what a guy. Honestly, what a legend. He helped keep me going after Jordan left. I loved him to bits. He was one of the lads, who loved his sport and was an all-around good human who was warm, generous and radiating good vibes. He'd always be up for a lager in the evening, hanging with the group, never went to bed early like an old fart. He really embraced the energy Jordan and I brought, and said to us, 'You two are making this experience way more fun.' That meant a lot. It really did. We were a trio for a bit, a little brotherhood.

Paul Danan was another legend. He had been through some really tough stuff in his life but had bags of charisma. He walked in with that high energy and was always smiling and laughing. He did have a couple of clashes with some of the other housemates, but I got it – he was passionate, so fireworks were inevitable. Paul was expressive. When something upset him, he wanted to talk about it. Some people might've seen that as bitching or stirring. But I didn't see it that way. I think he was just a passionate guy who'd been taught not to bottle things up. And that's not a bad thing. He spoke from the heart. That said, I actually put him up for eviction, which I felt awful about afterwards. That was one of my worst moments in there.

Coming out of that show was the first time I stopped feeling like I was just Louise's little brother. More people started to take notice of me. I finished third and honestly, I think that's the best place to come. I was so happy because being third means you've done well, but there's less pressure than being the winner. You've done the show, people think you're all right and you move on. Nice and easy. I had the best time. I had always LOVED *Big Brother* – how could I say no? It was such a great opportunity to sit in that iconic chair. I loved it.

In fairness, no one remembers you being on CBB. But at least you had a great time

I WISH I'D DONE *SAS: WHO DARES WINS* WHEN I WAS A BIT OLDER, AS I DIDN'T TAKE IT SERIOUSLY ENOUGH

Sam

Another amazing show we both did – at different times – was *Celebrity SAS: Who Dares Wins*. I did the first series and, looking back, I made the huge mistake of going into it thinking I was gonna have fun. But no sooner was I in than

I quickly realised, Holy shit, this is not the kind of place you come to have fun. Because I'd been on *Big Brother* and a few light entertainment shows, I thought I could swan in and just be me.

Pete
Which is what no one wants to see. I mean, what a fucking show that was! And unlike stupid-bollocks, I really took it seriously. Honestly, along with *Celebrity Island*, it was one of the best shows I've ever done. I loved it. That's proper telly, that. No glam, no script, just raw, brutal stuff. And I was lucky enough to do it twice.

The first time was a fucking disaster as I ended up having to withdraw after I knocked myself out and broke some ribs during a challenge. Luckily, I was asked back and jumped at the chance. I wanted to test myself. I'd been living in this world of reality TV, blagging it, just surviving. I needed something different. Something properly physical and mental. Just to see if I was still the same bloke I was before all of this kicked off.

Sam
And what did you discover about yourself?

Pete
Well, it was a lot different the second time round. I was in a completely different headspace. Life had changed for me. The first time, I wanted to know if I could physically do it. The second time was mentally tough as I'd just lost my nan. I spoke about a lot of stuff. Left a lot of anger on that show. It got proper real.

That was the start of it all, really. *SAS* was what pushed me to write my last book. It made me realise that I hadn't dealt with a lot of shit. It's been a rollercoaster. Ten years of madness. And behind all that, loads going on personally.

You start to forget who you are underneath it all, know what I mean?

Sam
When I did it, I knew it was going to be tough, but I hoped I would bring the fun to the show. So I walked in, all smiles, like, 'Hey everyone, we're gonna have such a laugh! Who's gonna be my buddy?' I completely misjudged the tone.

Pete
You really are a knob!

Sam
Well, it was the first series, I had nothing to compare it to. I didn't know what was expected!

Pete
SAS: Who Dares Wins? What do you think you were going to be doing? Crochet?

Sam
Well, I thought it was gonna be like *I'm a Celeb* or something – bonding, tasks, have a bit of a giggle. But I soon realised it was nothing of the sort!

I kept calling Ant Middleton 'mate' and one time he went ballistic at me, screaming *'What the fuck?'* I was like, 'Oh my God! What the hell is going on here?' So I went, 'Sorry, mate.' And he shouted 'Call me mate again!' I started panicking, going, 'I can't stop calling you mate – I'm so sorry, mate!' He goes, 'You think you're funny?' And I'm just like, 'I don't even know if I'm being funny or not, I'm just panicking!'

Pete
He must have hated that.

Sam

Looking back, one of my biggest regrets is doing *SAS* when I did. I wish I'd done it when I was a bit older, because I didn't take it seriously enough. I just wanted to enjoy it. I love people. I love being around energy. I'm a big camaraderie person. But it just wasn't the right show for that.

Pete

Yeah, I'd love to see how you'd cope in there now. You'd probably be even worse!

Sam

One of the exciting things about being on the show was that I got to hang out with legends like Wayne Bridge. As I'm a massive Chelsea fan, I was desperate to be mates with him. But it's hard to be pals when you're carrying a 20kg Bergen up a mountain while being screamed at. I was dying, but I was still turning round, going 'Bridgie! Bridgie!' I'd also lie in the bunk beds whispering, 'Bridgie, can I join you?'

Pete

You did what?

Sam

I asked if could join him in his bunk.

Pete

And what did he say to that?

Sam

Well, he'd be like, 'I'm trying to sleep.' And I'd say, 'Do you mind if I just sort of lie at the end of your bed?'

Pete

So it's not just me you're weird with, then.

Sam

The experience was great, but that was another show where I got a bit of public hate. Some people liked me, but quite a few were like, 'He's just a little prick.' In retrospect, I do feel like I let myself down a bit.

Pete

Well, at least you're consistent. But if I recall, you did get pretty far in the show. Further than me, in fact, which pisses me right off.

Sam

Yes, I did. I was a skinny little runt, and yet I still almost made the final four. I think Bridgie still would've won.

Everyone thought I wasn't taking it seriously. But it wasn't that. It was just my way of staying sane. I didn't make the final four – in the end I handed my badge in as I kept making mistakes in our 'fake' hostage story. I was letting my team down so, for them, it was my time to go.

Pete

That's actually a good name for a spin-off pod! I'll write that down.

Sam

I try to have a laugh – that's what I do when I'm uncomfortable. I felt misunderstood by the public. I remember thinking, I don't get it, I haven't done anything wrong, but I was still getting heat.

And that's when I realised that audiences are made up of different kinds of people. Some who want to be entertained in a light way and others – especially with a show like *SAS* – who want to see real grit. And I totally respect that. But it took me a while to understand.

Pete

So what did we get from this experience? I dealt with my emotions about losing my nan, and you realised that carrying on like a gibbering twat can get on people's wick.

Sam

So, lessons have been learned!

Pete

Have they? Have they really?

Sam

And we saw how valuable brand-building was. We learned that by getting out there and appearing on shows like these you open yourself up to whole new audiences and catch the eye of producers on other shows. But you also have to understand how to behave on them, because certain shows attract certain kinds of viewers who might not tolerate a clown fooling about.

BUILD LDN WAS ONE OF THE MOST PIVOTAL TIMES IN MY LIFE

Sam

Over the past few years I have been lucky enough to be doing a lot of presenting on TV and hosting my own radio show. I can honestly say I am living the dream. But achieving these goals didn't happen overnight. One of the most important gigs I landed was hosting *BUILD LDN*, the YouTube interview series, which I did during a break in *Made in Chelsea*. In the States, the show was massive – it attracted some of the biggest stars in the world. I'd actually been on the UK version a few times as a guest, so to come back as the host was a really proud moment for me.

My brilliant agent at the time had got me a meeting

with a guy called Jeff Goodwin. He was looking for a new lead presenter and I was well up for it. So I went in for a test. I was obviously very green, but think I was good at it. Some of the other people doing test reads were a lot more experienced – not necessarily more talented, but definitely more polished.

Fortunately for me, this was a time when companies were just starting to realise they needed someone with talent, but also a profile and a social media presence. I did the reading, and did all right. It was the first time I'd ever done anything like that. Then the next day, we got a call from Jeff. He said, 'Look, I'm going to take a punt on you. I want you to be the guy.' It was such a big deal for me. I was absolutely over the moon.

When I started on the show, it felt like such a huge step. We did some amazing interviews with big stars, like the cast of *X-Men* or whichever high-profile film or series was about to come out. The show was broadcast live, digitally, and we had a studio audience too. It was the first time I ever had to read an autocue. We had a gallery. I had an earpiece. It was so professional.

I still remember the opening line: 'Hello and welcome to *BUILD Series London*, live from the . . .' whatever venue we were in. 'I'm Sam Thompson.' And then the studio audience of about fifty fans would go 'Woo!' for whoever we were interviewing. It was a proper operation.

It was an amazing experience. I did a full year of it, basically learning on the job as a presenter. I learned so much. Whatever I am now, I owe so much of that to *BUILD* and to Jeff.

But no one really knows about those formative years of mine away from *MiC*, and how much time I was putting in. I kept it real quiet. But that year was probably one of the most important times in my whole career, learning my trade and gaining media experience. I still credit it as one of the most pivotal times in my life. It helped me rebrand myself as a presenter and opened me up to more opportunities.

'DON'T WORRY, YOU'LL ALL GET YOUR MOMENT. BUT THIS IS MY TIME'

Sam

The first time I did *Celebs Go Dating* was in 2018, just after Tiff and I broke up. The show was fun, but it taught me something big about staying relevant as a fledgling reality star – that there are levels to this game. At the start of filming me and some of the cast were all down in the basement at the agency, waiting to start. Then a well-known reality star walked in and announced, 'You lot are lucky I'm here.' At first I thought they were joking. They said, 'Don't worry, you'll all get your moment. But this is my time.'

Pete
Classic.

Sam

But mate, they weren't wrong. They brought the eyeballs to the show. Proper star power. I remember just thinking, Bloody hell … there's levels to this game and I'm nowhere near!

What I came to realise was, when you're in a show like *Made in Chelsea*, you're in a bubble. You might think you're a big deal because people know your name in SW3, but step outside of it into the wider world and you realise you're no one. Just a tiny fish in a big reality TV pond.

It was a wake-up call. I realised I wasn't even on the radar. It was a proper eye-opener. But you know what? Getting dumped on *Made in Chelsea* basically made my career.

Pete

Which particular dumping are we talking about? There were loads.

Sam

Exactly! Tiff dumped me, Sophie gave me the boot ... and on that second *Celebs Go Dating*? That's when I met you. If I hadn't been getting binned off left, right and centre, we wouldn't be sitting here now.

Pete

So you're telling me, if one of those girls had really liked you, you wouldn't be in my life?

Sam

I guess so.

Pete

Fuck me!

10

Getting Noticed

So we'd made ourselves a name on the telly. But you can't rest on your laurels. You need to keep yourself out there to make sure the press and public know you're still alive. Which means you have to try every which way to stay in the public consciousness.

I STILL COME OUT IN A SWEAT WHEN I HIT THE CARPET

Pete
The first time I did a red carpet was hilarious. I had a lazy eye as a kid, so standing in front of twenty photographers screaming 'This way! That way!' was chaos. The first few times, I swear I could see round corners. My eyes were going in different directions trying to look at everyone.

I never practised poses. I mean, do I look like the sort of bloke who practises poses? I guarantee you Sam does.

Sam
Well, I did to start with. I always wanted to make sure I flashed the right pose. I learnt a lot from my sister. But then I've had a few bad experiences on the red carpet, so never feel fully confident.

Pete
Do you remember your first one?

Sam
Yeah. It was with my sister. I totally panicked and ended up holding her handbag in the photo. Just stood there like a spare part – but I was buzzing to have been invited as I rarely got asked to anything. I remember trying to get into an In The Style party once and being turned away.

Pete
In The Style? Why would you be allowed into something like that? What do you know about style?

Sam
A lot, actually, since I hired my own personal stylist.

Pete
Don't get me started on that. Hundreds of quid for someone to stick you in a white T-shirt. My one-eyed Peggy could do a better job at styling you!

Sam
Your one-eyed Peggy? Sounds like you're talking about your cock!

Pete
That's fucking sick! So, anyway, what's this In The Style thing?

Sam
Oh, it's a fast fashion company. They used to book loads of celebs to front their range of clothes.

Pete
But not you!

Sam
Of course not me. I looked awful back then.

Pete
No arguments!

Sam
Anyway, when they tried to turn me away, I told them Binky Felstead's PR had invited me and they just went, 'You're not on the list.' I walked away so embarrassed.

Pete
Maybe you should have turned up wearing a T-with 'Louise Thompson's Brother' written across it.

Sam
I was always that guy outside the rope going 'Why doesn't anyone want me?'

Pete
What a fucking sob story!

Sam
And the worst part? Now I actually legitimately get invited to these things, I still come out in a sweat when I hit the red carpet. I don't even know how to smile.

I CAN'T STAND NETWORKING – LET'S TALK ABOUT DOGS INSTEAD

Pete
Showbiz parties and big events might look fancy, but

they're not really about having fun. They're about networking. Z-listers like us love these things, 'cos we can get pissed and remind the press and the public we are still alive. That's what Sam does.

Sam
I *love* a party! You can catch up with mates.

Pete
If they were real mates, you'd see them in your own time and not just at a free bar.

Sam
I do, but it's just nice to bump into mates you don't expect to. It's a nice bonus.

Pete
Well I for one swerve it when I can. Sam hates how I'll walk into a party, park myself at the bar, not move all night and somehow have everyone end up around me. No networking, just chatting. He's baffled.

Sam
Well, I'm all for chatting.

Pete
But the truth is, I don't care. I'm just there for a good time. Free bar? Let's get drunk – that's the vibe. I can't stand all that networking bollocks. People coming up to you, saying, 'So, what've you got coming up?' And I'm like, 'Nothing, mate. I'm having a tequila. I don't care. Let's talk about dogs.'

If you say you've got nothing going on, people go quiet and look sympathetic. So you have to do the whole 'Oh, there's stuff in the pipeline . . .' It's bollocks.

But – and this is good advice for any walk of life – if you're actually good at what you do, there's space for everyone. People aren't stopping you. You're stopping yourself if you get bitter about losing out. If someone else gets it? Be better next time.

But back to networking. I really can't be arsed with it. All that clout-chasing and picture-taking. I've never asked anyone for a photo. Sam asks everyone. But to be fair, it's not for clout. He's just a fan. He genuinely loves it. Sam's got imposter syndrome. He's always like, 'I can't believe I'm here.' Which is actually a lovely quality.

Sam

Awww, cheers mate! Highlight that. I want to remember it for ever.

Pete

Sam forgets he's on TV. He meets new Love Islanders and loses his mind. I'm like, 'Mate, you host part of that show.'

Sam

I can't help it. I watch the show, I get to know them, and I feel really invested in their story, so when I do meet them I'm buzzing and it's like, 'Wow! I know you! Can we be mates?'

Pete

Whereas me? I don't watch anything. But even if Denzel Washington sat next to me in a restaurant, I'd think, 'That's cool, I love Denzel,' but I'd carry on eating my dinner.

11

Imposter Syndrome

The public might know our names, our faces might be splashed across the press, but when we find ourselves in the company of proper actors, singers, talented people, there's a tendency to feel like we don't belong, and we begin to experience imposter syndrome. Until that glorious moment when we become what some might consider credible.

Pete
As we write this book, it's kind of weird to acknowledge that we have come a long way from our humble beginnings.

Sam
Haven't we just. Pete! We're podcasters, mate. Presenters. Arena-fillers. TikTok superstars.

Pete
Superstars, I'm not sure – let's not rewrite history. We came from the dregs of showbiz, managed to build careers off the back of very little and have been blagging it ever since.

Sam
Fair.

Pete

I mean when we went to events we were literally walking the red carpet with proper serious people. Like actors and pop stars. Real legends. And we were like, what are we doing here? I still feel that now. And the weird thing is, people like us, ones who have come from reality shows, probably get more reaction from the crowd than some of those other people, right? It's fucking embarrassing.

Sam

We get embarrassed by it, but it's beautiful, fucking beautiful... but I don't think it'll ever stop feeling weird.

Pete

Even though I'm on the telly, I've never considered myself a celebrity. I suppose I am one – reluctantly. But I don't think that feeling will ever leave me. Of course, things have changed a bit, especially after I was on *Strictly* and Sam was on *I'm a Celeb*. Now we kind of feel more comfortable being out there in the public eye. I don't feel like such a fraud.

Sam

Appearing on those high-profile shows that the country actually stop to watch has changed the way we've been perceived by the public, the media and TV bods. In a way, we feel legit, like proper stars, not just desperate wannabes trying to climb the ladder.

Pete

And because of that shift in perception we get offered to do more stuff that again legitimises who we are. Like when I was asked to do *The Real Full Monty* to raise funds and awareness for cancer charities. I was chuffed to be asked to help such a good cause. Same when it comes to the dog charities I've worked with.

Sam
And when I was asked to do the UNICEF challenge for Soccer Aid, I was so proud to think people thought I was a worthy enough person to represent this world-renowned charity. Did I ever think that would happen, when I was getting pied left, right and centre on *Made in Chelsea*? Course not. No one took me seriously back then! It was just a dream to think I could become – or at least feel like – part of the telly establishment.

Pete
But we can say this now. It hasn't always been this way. In the early days, we didn't feel like we belonged. We would walk the red carpet alongside proper stars looking down their snouts at us. But I guess it's a celebrity rite of passage.

Sam
So true, mate. No one is really born super-famous and credible.

Pete
Unless you're a nepo baby!

Sam
I mean, look at Dua Lipa. She used to work as a bouncer before she was a success. And Ed Sheeran started out in kids' theatre. They had to work their magic to get to where they are today. So feeling like an imposter is nothing to be ashamed about.

YOU START THINKING, DO I EVEN BELONG HERE?

Pete
I was on a judging panel once, where a big star was a bit of an arse and it's stuck with me. I won't name names. But . . .

it was a man who I fucking love, always have. When I turned up for this gig, he looks straight at me and in front of everyone goes, 'Why the fuck is he here?'

Sam

Fuck no! That must have been tough, seeing as you worship him.

Pete

He could have been joking, or maybe it was just one of those offhand comments, but it hit hard.

Sam

Why? 'Cos he hurt your feelings? That's not like you.

Pete

No, I've heard worse, but it got to me because it actually tapped into the doubts I carry around with me. You look around a room like that, see the names, the faces, and you start thinking, Do I even belong here?

Sam

Did you hit back with a trademark Pete Wicks verbal jab?

Pete

You know what I'm like – I bit back and said something like, 'Well, I suppose you're only funny when the camera's on.' Not my sharpest comeback, but it did the job. He actually laughed, which made me feel better, so it was sweet in the end, and we ended up getting on well. But that's always been me. If you come for me, I'll come back. Doesn't matter who you are. Still, that shit stays with you. It chips away a bit.

There was another time, when me and Megan did *Celebrity Juice*, not long after we'd split on *TOWIE*. The story had gone everywhere. Everyone knew. One of the games on that episode was a spoof *Mr and Mrs*, and someone clocked the 'loyal' tattoo on the back of my neck. Straight away it was like, 'Sorry, does that say "loyal" on the back of your neck?' And the audience pissed themselves laughing.

I know there was no harm behind it, but in that moment I felt a bit hurt, if I'm honest. I wanted to say something smart, but I let it slide. Then later there was another near the knuckle comment which had the audience wetting themselves. I'm all for a laugh, but being a reality TV bloke makes you an easy target, and when it's joke after joke at your expense, and you're not feeling your best, it does get you down.

So I waited, bided my time, then fired back and made some funny comment, but it was still heavy. I felt like I was being laughed at just because I was off a reality show There's been loads of moments where I've thought, What the fuck am I doing here? But at the end of the day, I count myself lucky to even be in those rooms.

Sam

Same with actors. I think there's a belief that just because we played out our lives on camera on our reality shows, we'll do anything to stay in the public eye and will do whatever is required.

Pete

Which I guess we all have done at some point. It's part of the job! Again, it's all about how to stay relevant. I reckon it must be hard for proper actors and singers to see people famous for having a barney on a reality show getting screamed at like they're the Beatles. I mean, there have been times when I've felt embarrassed as I've been getting more attention than a proper A-lister. But it's only because the press know we'll give them an easier ride. Or actually speak to them!

Sam

Pete and I, we're not trained in anything. It's only recently we've become presenters. So when you get more attention than people who've actually worked their whole lives for it, yeah, I get why that pisses people off. And you do get looked down on.

Pete

It's only really in the last couple of years that I've felt like I'm 'allowed' to be here. I've definitely learned skills that I never expected to. Writing is one of them. Like, I write all our live shows. I never thought I'd do that. It's not something I ever aimed for, I just thought, Fuck it, let's give it a go.

Sam and Pete's Rules for Surviving Imposter Syndrome

RULE 1: Everyone's winging it – some just fake it better.

RULE 2: You can't train to be famous – but you can learn not to be a dick.

RULE 3: Blagging isn't shameful – it's a skill.

RULE 4: If someone comes for you, bide your time – then hit back and be better than them.

RULE 5: Whether you're an established, successful actor or fresh off *Love Island*, everyone deserves the opportunity to be appreciated. If people are interested in you, who cares what it's for?

RULE 6: Stick around long enough and the proper stars will begin to admire you for your staying power and authenticity, and will see you for more than they originally thought.

RULE 7: Remember that everyone shits!

12

Divas

In every walk of life there are people who think they're a cut above the rest. While they might strut around with their hooter in the air, more often than not we all see right through them. But we have proven that by staying true to yourself and treating others with kindness and respect, you can go a long way!

Pete
It's not just the big stars with proper talent who can make you feel like dirt on the bottom of their shoe – plenty of people who started as low down the ladder as me shrug off their imposter syndrome and suddenly transform into full-on divas, complete with nasty strops. And that does my fucking nut.

When you work in TV, you can't really have an off day. You can't be like, 'Nah, can't be arsed today.' If someone's daft enough to pay me to do something, I'll turn up and give it 100 per cent, every single time. I've always had a strong work ethic.

Sam
Most definitely. If we say we'll do something, we do it. Work is work.

Pete
I don't do sick days. If I say I'll be there, I'll be there. The problem is a lot of people in this industry just don't have that mindset. Some of them are lazy as fuck. No respect at all. They just don't show up. No warning. Cancel last minute like it's nothing.

Sam
Thing is, in some normal jobs, if you call in sick often the place still runs. But in the TV world, if you're the focus of a shoot and you cancel, everything gets ruined.

Pete
You've got photographers, make-up artists, directors, producers – loads of people relying on that day – and it gets wasted. You can't just slot someone else in. What are they gonna do, wheel in a cardboard cutout? You're not just messing up your own schedule, you're screwing over everyone else's. That's why I don't cancel. I can't.

HOW TO STAY RELEVANT BY NOT BEING A SELF-CENTRED CELEBRITY

Pete
I've turned up to jobs before, stood around for an hour waiting and then they just cancel. That's my whole day gone. No shoot, no work, no pay. And honestly? It makes me want to go round to their house and give them a stern talking to. Because it's not just rude, it's selfish.

Sam
This industry is weird. Really weird. The funny thing is, on every show I've done, I've always got on best with the people behind the camera. The ones who actually make the

show – lighting, sound, make-up, cameras – they're the ones doing the graft.

Pete
We're just the dickheads in front of the lens, pretending to be interesting. Half the time I sit there thinking the crew must look at us and think, You absolute wanker. And I wouldn't blame them. I click with the crew because they're just normal people. Down to earth. Not up their own arse.

Sam
You turn up somewhere and people are like, 'Can I get you a coffee?' And I'm thinking, Don't be silly, let me get you one.

Pete
But I've seen people say, 'Yeah, I'll have this, I'll have that,' and not even look the person in the eye. Makes me mad.

Sam
I can't bear people like that. And we've seen our fair share over the years.

Pete
But you see what happens when people get that kind of treatment all the time. It can change them. Except for Sam, who I can safely say will never be up his own arse and throw his weight around!

Sam
No, I'll come bouncing into the room hugging everyone I meet and ask them to be my mate. Or get 'em a coffee. I meet people and think the best of them until they show otherwise.

I have, hand on heart, never had a diva strop. And the reason why? Because I remember exactly where I came from and I know that Pete and I are only where we are today because the people who follow us and like us have helped us get here.

Pete
Also, we know all this can be lost in the blink of an eye. And to use an old phrase, be good to the people on the way up, 'cos they could end up being your boss on the way down!

Sam
Amen!

KNOW THE DIFFERENCE BETWEEN POPULARITY AND NOTORIETY

Pete
Me and Sam, we've been around a while now. You see some new ones come in, all excited, asking for advice, being all polite and eager. Fast-forward six months and they're walking around like they're Brad Pitt. And if they're not careful they will lose everything they've achieved because people just won't want to work with them. I don't think they get the difference between popularity and notoriety. They think they're loved but really they're just known for being loud, or chaotic, or messy. That's notoriety. That's not the same as being liked. But they don't see it. And, slowly, they lose touch with reality.

Sam
It doesn't help that the press, the people around them, even the fans help feed them this idea. And before long, they've got no idea who they are any more. It's wild. Don't get me wrong, there are good people. But we've seen some mad shit over the years.

Pete

But look, it's not black and white. Good people do shit things. Bad people can have good days. It's complicated.

Sam

But some people can lose themselves in all this – and that's mad, when you think about it. You're getting paid to be yourself, and yet somehow you forget who you are.

TALENT DOESN'T ALWAYS GET YOU IN THE SPOTLIGHT – CONTROVERSY DOES

Pete

But it's not a great way of doing so

Do you know what the saddest part about being a reality star is? That being a prick doesn't stop you from getting work. It can actually make you stay relevant!

Nice guys don't always win. I know a couple of geezers off reality shows who are 'too nice' to be on other shows. They know that people are fascinated by how much of an arsehole some people can be. For me, that's the dark side of fame, and it doesn't sit well with me at all. But sadly they're the kinds of people that viewers tune in for. I mean, we're all aware of the telly stars who make a living out of being a diva and people piss themselves 'cos it's funny to watch, but imagine if you had to deal with someone like that in real life. It'd be a nightmare. No disrespect to any of them, they're just playing the game.

Sam

Viewers want to get caught up in the madness, so producers tend to cast characters who are divisive and can create moments that will go viral, so everyone is talking about it the next day. That's what it comes down to.

Pete
But is it right? No. Absolutely not. There are so many good people – genuinely good people – who've done reality TV or tried to, and they get overlooked. You can be the most talented person out there, but if you don't fit the brief a producer is looking for – you're not a six-foot model, or you can cause tension – then you get passed over for those who do fit the bill.

Sam
As a society, we love to watch chaos. Doesn't mean everyone on the show is awful, it's just the drama we're after. That's what reality TV thrives on. So if you're not bringing that, if you're just there going, 'Oh, I like everyone', you may not last. Some good guys are popular for years – like *MiC*'s Proudlock, for example. He's big in fashion now!

Pete
A lot of reality stars think they need to be extra and so they change the way they act to make sure they create enough drama to keep them relevant on the show. They become what they think people want to see, instead of just being who they are. But the thing is, you're lucky to get paid to just be yourself. So do that. Don't fake it.

Sam and Pete's Golden Rules for Surviving Reality TV and Life

1. Turn up. No excuses.
   No one cares if you're tired or hungover. If you're booked, turn up. Simple.

2. Always give 100 per cent, even when you can't be arsed.
   If you don't bring your A game, everything falls apart – and you'll be the person everyone hates.

3. Treat everyone with respect.
   The proper grafters are behind the scenes, the unsung heroes. They're the ones who make you look good.

4. Ditch the diva attitude.
   Don't chuck tantrums, don't make dumb demands. If you think you're too good to get your own coffee, you're in the wrong game.

5. Keep your feet on the ground.
   You might think you're a superstar whizz-kid, but you're not. You're just like the rest of us. Stay humble or you'll get a bad rep.

6. Don't play a character.
   Stop trying to be someone else – the public can see right through you.

7. Fame can be a flash in the pan.
   Enjoy it while it lasts.

8. Don't be a dick to newcomers.
   Everyone was new once. And who knows? They might end up your boss one day.

9. Never forget your roots.
   You were a kid with big dreams – never let go of that spark. It's what made you who you are today.

10. Find a best mate.
    Life can be a mad journey – find someone who gets you and sticks around when it all goes tits up!

— Just like us

YOU NEED TO REALISE WHERE YOU ARE IN THE GRAND SCHEME OF THINGS

Sam

I've got to be honest, one of the things that made me quit *Made in Chelsea* was the way some of the cast treated the crew. Like, properly awful. I saw runners in tears. And that never sat right with me.

But when you're in the bubble of a reality show and you're doing well in it, everyone is telling you you're this and that, and you end up thinking you're this massive star. You feel important, or at least you're made to think you are. But if you think about it, shows like *TOWIE* and *Made in Chelsea* are only watched by a small fraction of the population, and a certain demographic.

Some people forget this and fall into the trap of thinking they're bigger than they actually are. I'm not above it – I've been there myself. I discovered that unless you venture out and do other things, you won't realise how small you are. And that's no way to stay relevant in this industry. You have to be seen, and you need to realise where you are in the grand scheme of things.

MICHAEL MCINTYRE TOOK SOME OF MY SWEATY CHEESE!

Sam

Most people I've met in this industry who are technically higher up the ladder than me have actually been lovely. All the *This Morning* folks, like Ben Shephard and Cat Deeley, are great. Josie Gibson too. Dermot O'Leary is flipping lovely – I still get messages from him every now and then, just checking in on me.

Another big star who has made me feel very welcome is Michael McIntyre. He is one of the nicest blokes in the world. I appeared on the pilot of *The Wheel*, and he had no idea who I was. Before we recorded the show he came into my dressing room and said, 'I've just done some research on you. I quite enjoyed your Instagram.' And I was like, 'My mum's a massive fan.' And he goes, 'Do you want to send her a little photo?' It was just so nice. I got rebooked for the show once it was greenlit, and that time he came in and said, 'I actually requested you personally.'

Then a while later, I landed a gig hosting the red carpet at the TV BAFTAs.

Pete

Or so he thought! He called me up, crying his heart out, saying 'Pete! Pete! I'm doing the BAFTAs red carpet!' The fuck he was.

Sam

I thought I was doing it for the telly. Turns out I was doing the digital hosting.

Pete

Were you even doing *that*?

Sam

My main job was to hand out cheese on the red carpet, with someone following me with a phone to post as a live social media link.

Pete

Cheese?!?

Sam

It was so embarrassing. I remember everyone just walking past me, obviously thinking, Who's this dude offering me cheese? It was genuinely humiliating, and I started to feel really shitty about myself. No one dared come near me – didn't give me a second look – except for Joe Swash, who's a lovely bloke. He bounced up to me, picked up some cheese, chewed it and then spat it back onto the paper, going 'Ugh, this is rank.'

Then, all of a sudden, I heard a voice calling 'Sam! Sam!' I turned around and it was Michael McIntyre. I'm like, 'Oh my God, you all right, mate?' And he goes, 'How are you, man? Why are you holding a plate of cheese?' I explained that I was doing the digital content for the BAFTAs and it was my job to offer celebs some sweaty cheese.

Michael just laughed and said, 'Oh, I'll have a piece.' So he takes one, introduces me to his wife and then heads inside, telling me he'll see me later. And I just stood there thinking, What a guy. I will never forget that. I'll always tell that story to anyone who'll listen, because I think good people deserve to be recognised.

Part 3

Becoming Relevant

13

When Sam Met Pete

We've been edging you for over 130 pages, but now we finally get around to giving you what you want. The chapter where we meet for the first time and, against all odds, become **Celebs Go Dating's** *most successful relationship to date.*

Sam
I guess this chapter might feel a bit redundant to those of you who listen to the pod, as you already know how we met.

Pete
Of course they fucking do, we bang on about it all the time.

Sam
So maybe we don't need to go down this road again ...

Pete
But here we are.

Sam
... but there might be readers who don't listen to the pod. Who picked this up because they saw me crowned King of the Jungle or saw you dancing in those tight pink trousers

on *Strictly*. They won't know any of it, or at least not the ins and outs of how we got here.

Pete
We are close. We are best mates. But just to be clear – there've been no ins and outs.

Sam
Shall we go back?

Pete
To when our eyes first met across a crowded room?

Sam
Well, as you might know, we met long before *Celebs Go Dating* was a booking in our agents' diaries.

Pete
So you keep telling me. Still can't remember you. Maybe it was that traumatic I blocked it out altogether.

Sam
Or maybe you're just a dick.

Pete
It's not that I'm a dick. You're just not that memorable.

Sam
You literally had your hands on my face.

Pete
All right, now it's starting to sound fucking weird.

Sam
But you did. You shaved my face.

Pete
I did. That's true. At a PR event. I shaved his face. Christ.

Sam
And we bonded! We got on well – I remember us laughing.

Pete
What's funny is that I was paid to be there and you weren't. When I turned up, they asked if they could shave me and I was like, 'Fuck off. No way.'

Sam
Guess who said yes?

Pete
Yep, Sam was there, begging 'Shave me, shave me, shave me!' So I said, 'Well, I'll shave him, then.' It tied in with the brand and seemed like a laugh.

Sam
So I lay back in this chair, looked up into his eyes and he started gliding the razor across my cheeks.

Pete
Trying to get rid of what bumfluff he had. At this point, I didn't really know him. I had heard of him – apparently, he was the biggest knob to ever come out of *Made in Chelsea*. Which is quite the achievement. So we're up close and personal, and I remember him touching my face while I was shaving his.

Sam
It was so smooth.

Pete
He's there stroking my cheeks, telling me I've got soft skin, while I'm trying to concentrate. I was like, I don't even know this bloke, why is he caressing me?

Sam
Just a beautiful moment.

Pete
Yeah. And once I'd done my contracted hour, I fucked off and completely forgot it ever happened. And then we met properly on *Celebs Go Dating*.

Sam
Er ... hang on, have you forgotten that we actually met again *before* that? In a nightclub?

Pete
No, I can't say I remember.

Sam
You should, I've reminded you about it plenty of times. Even on the pod.

Pete
Sam, do you honestly think I listen to half of what you say? I just let you think I do. So go on then, refresh my memory. Enlighten the readers: where we really first met.

Sam
This is so embarrassing for me.

Pete
That goes without saying.

Sam
About a month before we were due to start filming *Celebs Go Dating*, I bounded up to Pete in this nightclub and said, 'Hi Pete, I think you're doing *Celebs Go Dating* with me.' And Pete, who's at the bar with a couple girls on either side of him, says, 'Oh, cool.' So I said, 'So should we have a drink together or something?' And he's like, 'Yeah, all right, we'll have a shot.' So we did and chatted for a bit ... and then he just walked off. Then when we started filming, he acted like he'd never seen me before in his life.

Pete
I genuinely couldn't remember you. You're saying we were drinking? I imagine I had to, just to get through the pain of it.

When you showed up at *Celebs Go Dating*, you came bouncing in, jumped all over Tom Read Wilson, said hi to literally everyone and left me till last, then you hugged me like we were long-lost brothers or something. I had to say, 'Slow yourself down, son.' And then pretty much from there he just attached himself to me.

Sam
Yes, I bloody well did!

Pete
Boy, did he aggravate me. I mean, literally from day one. But Sam, I've told you before, my first impressions of you still haunt me. You see, when you do shows like that, there's always one tosser who's over the top, loud, talking constantly just for the sake of talking ...

Sam
Hello!!!

Pete

See? I remember sitting there thinking, Oh God, he's going to be a lot of energy. And within the first hour, I was like, 'Someone shut him the fuck up.'

Sam

But that's our origin story, for those who didn't know or for those who needed to be refreshed.

Pete

The first bit of filming we did for *Celebs Go Dating* was this thing where you go to a mixer. This is where you walk into a room full of fifty single women and just talk to them. Lucky fucking me, I was put in there with him. Now, that's a dream scenario. A room full of women and you're one of only two blokes in there? It's fucking brilliant, isn't it? Sam, though? Sam was petrified. Like, properly shaking.

Sam

Scared stiff!

Pete

You mean just scared. As we were about to go in, he went, 'Can I stand with you?' And I'm like, 'Not really, mate,' 'cos I didn't want him to cramp my style. He asked, 'So what do we do?' and I said, 'Just fucking walk in. We'll have a little scout, find a corner. You can't talk to fifty women at once. Get a drink, suss it out. And then ... just do the eyes.'

Sam

And I said, 'What do you mean, "do the eyes"?' Pete told me to make eye contact with someone I fancied, give 'em a look and then talk to them. But I'm not sure how to do the eyes, so asked what I should do, and he tells me, 'Just smile with your eyes, but don't be creepy about it.'

Pete

So what does he do when we get in there? He starts staring at people. And waving. I'm like, 'What the fuck are you doing? You look like you're having a medical episode.' So I left him to it and went off on my own. I don't know what Sam did, but I did hear later that he was starting every conversation with 'Who do you think would win in a fight, Shrek or a bear?'

Sam

And? Which would?

Pete

I'm not answering that! We have a whole podcast full of fucking hypotheticals. Or hy-pathetic-als. So yeah. Day one, advice ignored. But then, as the show went on, it kind of became a thing. He'd start asking for my advice on everything.

Sam

Yep, I was a bit of a tool with the ladies.

Pete

And I guess I became your unofficial mentor.

Sam

You know, when we met I knew we were polar opposites. But I also knew that we would make great TV together and that I'd have a laugh along the way. So I sneakily went up to the producers behind his back and begged them to put me with him. Then I set about coming up with funny situations to drop him in. All without him knowing.

Pete

What a total tosser!

Sam

The thing is, I love that stuff, creating little storylines. Honestly, half the time it felt like I was secretly directing and producing my own mini show inside the show.

Pete

Yeah, cheers for that, mate.

Sam

I used to literally whisper to the cameraman, 'Oi, mate, spin the camera round NOW, I'm about to say something and I know exactly what Pete's gonna do.'

Meanwhile, Pete's just there, totally oblivious, bless him.

Pete

Until right now, apparently.

Sam

Exactly! But that's why it worked. Pete would just be Pete. No acting, no filter. Pure TV gold. We're basically the bargain bin version of Ricky Gervais and Karl Pilkington ... except sometimes we're both Karl.

Anyway, my secret plan was to wear Pete down. And I did. Eventually.

Pete

But all the while I was thinking, I don't know if I can get through this whole series with this noisy prick. I thought, Surely he can't be like that all the time.

Six years later ... he is. And annoyingly, it's the thing I love most about him.

Sam

Aww, Pete!

Pete

Never in my wildest dreams did I think he'd end up becoming my best mate. Not just a mate, a brother. But during those first few weeks of filming? I'd have done anything to get away from him.

Sam

I'm like herpes, mate. You can take medication, but I'll still get back in there. I'm a flare-up.

Pete

A flare-up, and you're there for life. You can't get rid of it.

Sam

Doesn't matter if I'm on your lip or on your bollocks, I'm turning up.

Pete

It's in the bloodstream. And that's Samuel Robert De Herpes Thompson.

PETE LOOKED AT ME AND WENT, 'YOU'RE ACTUALLY LIKE THIS, AREN'T YOU?'

Sam

I was so determined for Pete and me to be proper bros that I told the producers, 'I want to be in every scene with him.'

Pete

And I went to the same producers and said, 'I can't do much more with him.'

Sam

We did this away day to Manchester, and I said, 'Can I share the train up with Pete?' They went, 'We'll film it.' I was like,

'Brilliant.' So it's just me and Pete on this train, cameras set up opposite us. And I go, 'Should we get a couple of lagers?' I had a lemonade as it was a bit too early for lager, really. But Pete ... well ...

Pete
I might have had one. I had to block this guy out somehow.

Sam
I'm there, going through stuff with Pete like, 'Mate, we're going to be dating, what do I even say to the girls? You're a proper ladies' man.' And I remember it so clearly, Pete looked at me and went, 'You're actually like this, aren't you?'

He said, 'I thought you were putting it on, but you're actually like this.'

Pete
That train journey to Manchester was about three and a half fucking hours. They filmed for about an hour, and I thought, All right, cool, that's done. Job's a good 'un. Then the cameras stopped. But Sam didn't. I said to him, 'Mate, they're not even filming this now.' And he goes, 'Yeah, I know.' So I said, 'Then shut the fuck up.'

I was trying everything to ignore him. I put on my headphones to listen to music, but he kept waving at me and asking if I was all right. And I'm like, 'Yeah, mate, yeah.' Headphones back in. Two minutes later: 'So what are we gonna do about the ...' And I'm thinking, For fuck's sake.

Sam
But then something happened. Something you didn't expect.

Pete
What?

Sam
That train journey was the turning point for Pete.

Pete
It was?

Sam
It was, because it was then that you started to realise you might actually like me. Isn't that right, my old mucker?

Pete
Well, let's just say, I didn't find you quite as much of a pain in the arse as I first thought. In fact – and I truly hate myself for saying it – I did like him. And why? Because he was the same on camera as he was off it. And in this industry, that's really fucking rare. Even though he was annoying – and believe me, he was doing my head in – he was just as annoying when the cameras weren't rolling. I actually appreciated that. He was unapologetically himself. You see when someone is totally genuine, not putting on any airs or graces. It doesn't matter if they're loud, chaotic, a bit much – if it's real, I respect that. We'd both been in the game a while, and finding someone who's just real? That's gold.

THAT WAS THE FIRST TIME SAM TOLD ME HE LOVED ME

Pete
When we arrived in Manchester, Sam and I and the rest of the celebs were whisked off to a speed-dating event. And what do you know? Old Sammy boy made sure he was sitting next to me.

The event started off all right. Some nice girls dropped by, but if I'm honest none of them really made much of an impression. Then halfway through, I noticed a girl sitting with Sam and it was clear that he was hook, line and sinker in love with her. In just two minutes. I couldn't help but smile at the way he was acting – like a bouncy puppy jumping around for some treats. He was in his element, and I heard him ask her on her date. He was so keen, it was almost painful to watch. But then I was pleased to earwig that she said yes. Good on Sam, I thought.

But alarm bells suddenly rang because as he was talking to her, I noticed that she kept giving me the eye, even though I was mid-conversation with my own date. Then when she moved across to my table for a two-minute date, she was practically yanking my trousers off with her eyes.

'So everything seemed to go quite well with Sam, then?' I said to her.

'Yeah ...' Okay, that's good, I thought.

'Are you going on a date with him now?' I asked, probing a little further.

'Well ... I mean, he's asked me on one,' she replied shiftily.

'And you accepted?'

She looked me in the eye. 'Well ... unless something else comes around.'

I knew where this was going, so pushed her a bit more. 'What do you mean?'

'Well, it wasn't Sam I had my eye on.'

'Oh yeah, who's your eye on?' I asked, with the intention of setting her up.

'You.'

'So what you're saying is,' I said coolly, 'if I asked you on a date, you'd go on one with me instead of Sam?'

'Yeah.'

I looked over at Sam and thought, 'How dare you ruin this for him?' Something suddenly switched in me, and I got properly protective. I told her, 'Well, unfortunately for you, he's my mate. I wouldn't do that. And I'll be telling him not to go on a date with you either.'

She looked shocked and said, 'What . . . ?'

I think she thought she was being really cool, but I didn't like her tactics.

Once the speed dating was over, I pulled Sam aside and said, 'She's not for you.' And he was like, 'What?' I told him, 'Don't worry about it. She's just not for you. Don't go on a date with her.' Although he didn't say it, I think he knew what had happened.

Sam
I did. I was gutted as I really fancied her.

Pete
I think that was the moment Sam knew I'd always have his back. And it's been like that ever since, really.

Sam
Aww, mate!

Pete
God, we sound like a couple.

Sam
Then we kissed. He said 'I love you' first.

Pete
You could say that was the moment where 'Sam and Pete' really became a thing. Because from then on – and this was pretty early in the series, only a few weeks in – we did pretty much everything together.

Sam
We even ended up getting the final scene.

Pete

Which is usually the one where they show people who've actually met someone. Except in our case, it was Sam telling me how much he loved me and me telling him I loved him.

Sam

But there wasn't exactly a happy ending, was there, Pete?

Pete

What he means is that after the show I blanked him for bit.

I HID IN A BIN AND POPPED OUT WHILE PETE WAS TRYING TO WORK

Sam

So yes, after we wrapped on *Celebs Go Dating* Pete didn't call me. I thought we had forged this amazing bond and that we would be hanging out together every day for the rest of our lives. We had shared so much and got so close, I reckoned Pete wouldn't be able to stay away. But the fucker didn't call or anything.

Pete

You see, what normally happens is that people get really close during the making of a show, then when it's over the bond just fades. I've done loads of shows and you always get that 'Let's start a WhatsApp group!' energy. The minute I finish filming, I mute the WhatsApp group. It's not because I don't like people – I've made some very real, lasting friendships on these shows – but everyone's moving on to the next thing.

Sam

I love to follow what they are doing.

Pete
Sounds creepy! People get busy. Life gets busy. So I just assumed that was that. But Sam was... persistent. A couple of weeks later, he randomly called me.

Sam
I remember that phone call. Pete didn't pick up the first time, so I called him again. He answered with 'What do you want?' And I was like, 'Well, we haven't spoken since *Celebs Go Dating*... I just wanted to catch up, really. How are you, mate? What's going on?'

Pete
If I'm really honest, Sam probably wouldn't have become my day-to-day mate had he not harassed me. It was all him. I've never had a male friend like Sam. I've never wanted one. I can't remember how it all spawned from there, really, but he just wouldn't leave me alone.

Sam
Well, I'd drive all the way to east London, to where he had the fashion business he ran with his mate Jake Hall, just to hang out with him. And then I'd do like twenty Instagram stories in a row, just following him round for the 'gram. I even hid in a bin once, and popped out while he was trying to work.

Pete
Fuck me! Can you see what I had to put up with?

Sam
He'd go to the loo and I'd follow him, film him having a shit. I filmed everything he did. I was obsessed. I remember thinking, God, I could do this for the rest of my life – just follow Pete around with a camera and be there every second.

Pete

And that's what he's done. So, Sam, why was I your obsession?

Sam

I was going through a big change in my life. I'd just been dumped, for, like, the third time. I had really low confidence. So *Celebs Go Dating* came at the perfect time. I've always been looking for a guy friend I could look up to. I've never had a brother, never had that sort of relationship, and I really needed someone to lean on, someone I could grow with. Then Pete walked in and changed everything.

> **WHEN THE SHOW ENDED, PETE TRIED NOT TO BE BEST MATES. BUT I WAS LIKE, 'FUCK YOU, I'M CALLING YOU EVERY DAY'**

Sam

People always ask me, 'Is Pete really like he is?' And I'm like, 'Yeah, he's a complete wanker most of the time.' But underneath, he's got the biggest heart.

If I was ever in proper trouble, Pete would be my first call. Not my mum. Not my dad. Pete. And I know for a fact he'd do everything in his power to help me.

Pete

This silly fucker is going to make me cry.

Sam

When I went through some relationship difficulties, I told Pete I was overwhelmed. He came over, gave me loads of advice. And honestly, I saw from the moment I met him, he wasn't a dickhead. He's one of the good guys. Like Tony Bellew in the jungle. The people who are a bit stand-offish? They're usually the ones with the biggest hearts. The ones who've been through shit – they're the most genuine. I'm a bit of a complex fella.

Pete

Complex? You're about as complex as a game of snap!

Sam

I am. I'm up and down. I can be happy-go-lucky, then really fucking sad. But Pete? He's super level-headed. He's been through a lot. If you've read *Never Enough*, you'll know the struggles he's faced.

I've had it easy by comparison. But people who've had hard lives, especially young people, it forms them. Gives them layers. Pete probably needs therapy for it, but he's had so much life experience, and he's so self-aware, kind, grounded. I saw that in him instantly.

I was vulnerable and I thought, I'm going to be your buddy. I did the whole journey on the show with him. By the end, I was like, 'He's my best mate.' When the show ended, Pete tried not to be best mates. But I wasn't having any of it and was like, 'Fuck you, I'm calling you every day.'

IF I COULD BE HALF THE MAN SAM IS, I'D BE HAPPY

Pete

That's always been my reaction to anything emotional, whether it's relationships or friendships. When it starts getting serious, I bounce. I leave. I'm usually better on my own. But Sam didn't give me that choice. I tried to leave. He clung on. And I'm so grateful he did.

We always take the piss that we're the only successful relationship to come out of *Celebs Go Dating*, but it's true. It is down to the show. Sam's just said a bunch of nice things that make me feel fucking awkward, but honestly, I've grown not to want to do any of this without him. I wouldn't enjoy it half as much. And even though I thought I'd be the one helping him through stuff, guiding him – because, let's be honest, he's a bit of a donut – he's actually come full circle. To the point now where his opinion means more to me than almost anyone's. There are so many parts of Sam I wish I had. If I could be half the man he is, I'd be happy. That's the God's honest truth.

Sam
Which parts?

Pete
I mean, you're more selfish than I am.

Sam
Thank you.

Pete
But that's because I like to help people, fix things, because it makes me feel better about some of the stuff I've done. Fuck me, this is like therapy now.

Sam
Aw, mate!

Pete
If I'm being honest – and I will say this only once – I don't think I've met a kinder, more genuine, more accommodating person. He is the most patient person I've ever been around. He's patient with my moods, with other people's chaos. Sam. I've seen you grow over the past seven years, from an annoying little fucker ... to an annoying man. And that's a big thing. Because I think you've learned so much about yourself. You've found your direction.

Sam

I have, Pete. And you're a big part of that.

Pete

Honestly, I couldn't be prouder of you. I said it to you in the jungle. I'll say it again now: I'm proud of who you are. But more than anything, I'm proud that you chose to stick around and be my mate.

Sam

You don't make it easy.

Pete

You're probably the most constant thing in my life. And I'm very grateful for that. You give me stability. You make me a better person.

Sam

I'm speechless, mate.

Sam and Pete: *Celebs Go Dating*'s Greatest Love Story Ever Told

The show's Anna Williamson reminisces about the day she birthed our boys!

First impressions

I'll have to cast my tired, old perimenopausal mind back to when I first met them both. But here's what I remember ...

It was actually the first time I'd met either of them. And, funnily enough, my first day on *Celebs Go Dating* was also the day the boys met, so, genuinely, I was there at the birth of Sam and Pete. It all happened in the same scene. I'll never forget it. We were filming in one of the big agency rooms, and we'd set up a sort of brunch party.

The idea was to introduce me to the show, and for us all to meet each other. One by one each celeb would come into the room and join this big, dysfunctional family around the table.

Pete

When Pete walked in I remember thinking, Ah, this is Pirate Pete, the lothario, the love rat from the tabloids. I hadn't really watched *TOWIE*, but I was aware of this very handsome tattooed man with long hair, sort of pirate chic. The media had painted him as aloof, mysterious.

But here's the thing – and it's one of the reasons I love my job: I meet these people with some kind of preconception, but there's always a deeper story. So Pete comes in, and I remember sitting down and getting what I now call the 'Pete Wicks eyes'. Anyone who's ever had it knows what I mean. Pete has this incredibly expressive face. It's like a Superman laser stare. He unpacks people with his eyes. You can see the wheels turning.

From his eyes, I could immediately tell whether he was sizing someone up, flirting or being guarded. Pete wears his soul in his eyes. Not only are they beautiful, but they're revealing. And I could tell straight away he was thinking, All right, who's this bird in front of me? What's her deal?

But very quickly, I warmed to him and him to me. There was something going on behind those eyes. I thought, Here's a man with a hell of a lot happening beneath the surface. Cool, calm, suave exterior, but my instincts told me there was a soft little kitten inside. And then Sam walked in.

Sam

Sam was our last celeb to arrive that day. And you could *see* in Pete's eyes: What the hell is this?! Sam bounded in like an excitable chimp. Immediately I thought, Here's my guy. Sam reminded me of my younger brother – no filter, no awareness of social cues. And I mean that in the most affectionate way. Sam is so unapologetically *himself*. He wears his heart on his sleeve. You know exactly how he feels, all the time.

He came bursting into the room, arms wide open, hugging everyone. And Sam's hugs are quite something. If you've had one, you know they are *bear hugs*. Full-on, emotionally intense. And there they were: Pete on one side of me, all guarded and cool, Sam on the other, all heart and chaos. I thought, Pete is going to find him annoying as hell. And Sam is going to want to be his best friend. That dynamic was *immediately* fascinating.

Their union

Celebs Go Dating is quite a solo journey. You're really vulnerable. We, the dating agents, are very probing. So naturally the celebs tend to gravitate towards one another.

Bonds form fast. It's what we call the law of proximity: you spend intense time together, and friendships accelerate.

But Sam and Pete? No one could've predicted *that* pairing. Especially not in those early weeks. Pete was on his own trajectory. He was like a Gatling gun with the women. Brilliant ratings, all the way through. But the same consistent feedback kept coming up. And here's where I use my therapy speak: he was presenting as *avoidant*. Excellent at flirting. Elite level eye-f**king.

You honestly can't appreciate the effect Pete Wicks has on women until you witness it first hand, especially at a *Celebs Go Dating* mixer. It is *literally* knicker-dropping when Pete walks into a room. Paul Brunson and I said this since day one: we've never seen anything quite like it. The guy is magnetic.

He'd love it. He was very much on his own trajectory. We had our own challenges with him – commitment issues, emotional avoidance, all of it.

And then there was Sam, on his own little dating journey. He was his lovable, geeky self, completely unapologetic about his love for *Harry Potter*. They were *very* different daters. But what was always so apparent was that they were both incredibly kind men, with real emotional depth. And they showed up as themselves – no pretence.

Their defining moment

Then came what I'd call a defining moment, something that happens quite often on the show. It's that kind of 'sink or swim' moment. And I was really lucky, because I had a front-row seat to it.

It was the moment Sam and Pete *became* Sam and Pete, arguably the most heartwarming love story we've ever created.

At that speed-dating event, Pete could see what was coming, that Sam was about to be mugged off. And Pete *stepped in.* He went into big brother mode. He didn't want Sam to get hurt. So he gently pulled him aside and said, 'Look mate, just so you know, this is actually the situation.'

That was the moment Pete really *saw* Sam, his openness, his vulnerability. And he realised *this* is someone special. Someone honest. Someone he wanted to protect. And Sam, in turn, saw in Pete a brother figure. Someone to admire, yes, but more than that: someone who had his back. Sexy, suave Pete, stepping up for goofy, sincere Sam. In that moment there was this beautiful overlap, a kind of enmeshment of empathy, values and connection.

As Sam went on more dates, Pete became his cheerleader. He started acting as his unofficial wingman. And if you know Pete, you'll know he's a protector. He pours his love and loyalty into others, sometimes to the point of forgetting himself. He did that with Sam.

Pete is a classic people-pleaser and rescuer. He saw in Sam this beautifully innocent person, and he couldn't bear the idea of him being hurt. He really *invested* in Sam, his time, his energy, his care. And it was completely genuine. Sam, in turn, gave Pete something too. There was this mutual recognition of each other's value.

As the show continued, we started to see more physical affection between them. Sam, being Sam, would throw his arms around Pete, full-on hugs. At first, Pete was visibly uncomfortable. But over time you could see he secretly loved it. He just wasn't used to that kind of demonstrative male affection.

A chosen family

There was this lovely evolution – Pete going from 'What is this?' to 'I kind of need this'. Both of them started getting something they'd been missing. And suddenly, it was like, *you* complete *me*. They filled a friendship-shaped gap in each other's lives.

They realised they'd found a kind of brotherhood they'd never really had before. It was powerful.

Relationships evolve, especially friendships. And sometimes our friendships are *the* most important relationships in our lives. More important, even, than a romantic partner. As human beings, we are wired for connection, we're designed to *belong*. And Sam and Pete? They *belong* with each other. You saw it when Pete surprised Sam in the jungle. Or the way they've supported each other through different ventures. They are each other's biggest cheerleaders.

They're yin and yang. Just like me and Luisa Zissman on our *LuAnna* podcast, some dynamics just *work*. And over the years, Sam and Pete have become intrinsically linked, personally and professionally. They're a perfect example that family doesn't have to be blood.

What they've built is a chosen family. They've become each other's support system, non-judgemental, loyal, ride-or-die. They're walking side by side, through life and work. And the strength, the counsel, the bond they share? It's unbreakable.

The boys

Pete is such an emotionally mature man. He's a brilliant example of someone who's grown, and all for the better. I've always said he'll make an amazing husband and father when he chooses to fully let someone in. Sam is the same. He's just the most wonderfully loving guy.

And while they're both phenomenal individuals, together they're something really special. It's no surprise to me – or to Paul – that they became 'Sam and Pete'. They represent so much of what we either *have* in a best friend, or what we *aspire* to have. Their authenticity, their vulnerability, their humour . . . they bring all of it. And it's so real.

It's just so lovely to see two genuinely kind men succeed. It honestly couldn't happen to two nicer blokes.

On their single status

Pete has so many emotional defences up, and deep down, he's afraid. That fear is completely valid: he's afraid of being hurt or abandoned. What Pete really needs to do is start taking his own advice. He's incredible at guiding others, but he needs to give himself that same grace. He should try gradually letting someone in, bit by bit. And I think he needs to date outside the industry. Someone who matches him intellectually is important. He should step away from his usual dating patterns and try something different, something unexpected. Because he's got *so* much to offer. But until he believes that, until he truly sees his own worth in the context of a relationship, he'll keep self-sabotaging. But with time, I believe it will come.

Pete needs to *believe* it can happen. That's the key. One of my favourite quotes is 'Whether you think you can or you think you can't, you're right.' I think, right now, Pete doesn't fully believe he *can* meet someone who's truly right for him. And that belief becomes a barrier.

Sam needs to keep embracing that beautiful uniqueness of his. He's this lovable guy, unapologetically himself. He should look for someone who shares his passions, all the things he genuinely loves.

Sam, like Pete, needs to change *where* he's dating. He should be looking for love outside the bubble of celebrity and within spaces that really align with who he is. That authenticity is his superpower.

If they step outside the public eye when it comes to dating, that shift will give them the balance they need, light and shade between their personal and professional lives. That's vital. It all can't blend into one.

Pete is a classic avoidant attachment style, and Sam is classic anxious. They're so opposite ... and yet they're so good for each other.

There's nothing wrong with either attachment style. What matters is awareness. Once you understand your patterns, you can grow within them.

Pete

Well that was deep, Anna. But God, we love you – you are one of the most genuine people this industry has. And, quite simply, it was where it all started for all things 'Sam and Pete'.

Sam

We love you so much, Anna. I feel quite emotional, tbh.

14

Can't Fight the Chemistry

I DID *CELEBS GO DATING* FOR THE CASH – AND HAD A LAUGH

Pete
So, as you are aware, following my romantic blow-ups on *TOWIE*, I decided not to share any personal aspects of my life any more. So why, you ask, did I do *Celebs Go Dating*? Well, for the money, 100 per cent. Who wouldn't? I definitely wasn't looking for love. I mean, come on, it's called *Celebs Go Dating*, not *Celebs Find Love*. That's the thing: you're on the show with a bunch of people, but no one actually ends up together. I think Sam and I were the only ones who kind of did . . . which is weird in itself. Then somehow it just became a thing.

Sam
Oh yes, we became a thing. A duo, a twosome, a perfect couple.

Pete
To be fair, and I can't believe I'm saying this, it ended up being one of the most fun shows I've ever done. That's why I went back so many times. The second time wasn't just

for the money, it was genuinely a laugh. It's not meant to be serious – it's narrated by Rob Beckett, who's absolutely hilarious. The whole point is to take the piss.

I met loads of great people behind the scenes, too. That first time, I made some proper mates. Paul Brunson and Anna Williamson: they're brilliant. Proper smart, genuine therapists. And Tom Read Wilson, who's a good mate of mine now as well.

So yeah, I went back for the cash – no lies – but also because it's a fun, light-hearted show. No pressure. No one's pretending it's *Love Island*.

I wasn't there to find someone seriously. I just tried to make it funny, because that's how I saw it. And in the middle of all that you do meet some solid people. As much as I moan about some of the people in this industry, I've been lucky to meet some proper decent ones too.

And then there's Sam. He did the show twice. His second time was my first – so that's when I got lumbered with him. And really, I owe *Celebs Go Dating* for that.

15

Staying Relevant Begins

After years of trying to make it, and still not quite making it, we decided to look inward and poke fun at our messy journey, to see if anyone found it as funny as we did. But before the podcast you all know and love, we experimented with a couple of other ideas first...

Pete
The union between Sam and me basically became what *Staying Relevant* is today. We knew that we were – and I'll whisper this – great friends. We had good chemistry and the public liked to see us hanging out together. I'm sure there were still people out there who thought Sam was a bit of a *Made in Chelsea* wally and I was the arrogant prick off of *TOWIE*. So what could we do?

Release a rap record like Kem and Chris from *Love Island*?

Sam
Oh, that would be awesome. Can you imagine us spitting rhymes on stage?

Pete

No, Sam, I can't. So we had a really long, hard think.

Sam

A long hard, wank always gets the juices flowing.

Pete

Long, hard think, you tit. Anyway – and again I must give Sam his due – he came up with a short-lived TV show called *Reality News*.

IF WE WERE A PANTOMIME DONKEY, I'D BE THE REAR

Pete

As I've said, Sam is the ideas man. I'm in the back office, carrying the ideas man up the hill while he's telling anyone who'll listen about how we're gonna make it. The face of Sam and Pete is Sam. He'd be at the front, doing all the lines and everything else. How can I make this any clearer? If we were a pantomime donkey, I'd be the arse end! But anyway, the first thing we did was *Reality News*.

Sam

And do you know where the idea for that came from? Snoop Dogg used to do this spoof news show on YouTube. He presented a celebrity news show in a funny, anarchic way and would cut to weather bulletins which weren't actual weather bulletins, just some scantily clad girl twerking into the camera. Then it would cut back to him, and he'd carry on with the news as normal. And he got millions of views.

I realised no one was doing comedy reality TV news like that, and thought it would do really well as there was a gap in the market. So I pitched it to Monkey Kingdom, the production company behind *Made in Chelsea*, and they ran with it. They took it to E4, and we got the 11 p.m. slot.

Pete
Yep, we got the graveyard shift, and we were like, 'Oh well, that's fine, we'll take it.' We were told by the bosses that doing a show like this was a stepping stone, and it would help us work towards something else, something bigger in the future. So you can imagine how chuffed we were to be given an hour-long show at 11 p.m. on a Monday night.

Sam
Except it wasn't.

Pete
'You've just got fifteen minutes,' the producers told us. Fifteen minutes? Fuck me, I've had shits that lasted longer than that. Okay, great, so we we're doing an advert every Monday night. That was effectively it, and we did it for quite a while. The hope was that when the show was up and running, the offers would start rolling in.

Sam
But they didn't.

Pete
Yeah, Sam had been convinced we were going to Hollywood.

Sam
I thought we were going to be the new James Corden and do something like *The Late Show*. I thought *Reality News* was gonna be the springboard for us to go to the US and do our version.

Pete
So we did this series of eighteen episodes and, honestly, they were a lot of fun to film. Basically we did a fun take on what was happening in the world of showbiz. Nothing serious, just Sam and me doing pretty much what we do on the podcast.

Sam
Bantering back and forth, Pete pretending he hates me ...

Pete
Pretending?

Sam
As the series went on, we waited for something to happen, hoping someone would spot us and say, 'These two guys would be perfect for a big shiny-floor show on ITV.'

Pete
Yeah, but absolutely nothing happened. No offers. Nothing. So, with nothing else lined up – and let's be honest, it was paid work – we signed up to do another series of ten episodes. Then E4 came back and asked for a third, and we just went, 'Nope. Not doing that again.' That's why it stopped.

Sam
Actually, that's not entirely true. It's more embarrassing than that.

Pete
What's more embarrassing than hosting a fifteen-minute advert that about three people watched? And they only watched it 'cos they couldn't work their fucking remote.

Sam
We'd hired this producer to help us make the show. Lovely guy, who was properly invested in it. And he ended up getting promoted to commissioner at E4, primarily off the back of our show. So we're buzzing. We got along with him and were thinking, This is it! He's in the big chair now. We're getting the hour-long slot, better time, everything. Then I was on this recommission Zoom with Channel 4 and I asked him, 'So, how's it looking?' And he goes, 'I'm really sorry to tell you this, but I've had to cancel your show.'

Pete
That's showbiz.

Sam got so upset, but still somehow hopeful. Classic Sam. Me? I just went, 'Ah, fucking bollocks. It is what it is. We'll carry on.' You see, Sam does what he always does, he overthinks everything, goes and has one of his sit-down showers, which is his version of therapy. Loves a sit-down shower. And within a week? Comes back with *Staying Relevant: The Sitcom*.

I GENUINELY DON'T THINK THEY COULD'VE FOUND ANYONE WORSE TO PLAY SAM THAN SAM

Sam
So, with *Reality News* down the pan, we needed something else to work on. And then it came to me. Like Pete says: in the shower, while scrubbing my balls. A mockumentary sitcom, based on how ridiculous our lives in TV had been.

Pete
When he first told me, I said, 'I don't think anyone really wants to watch that.' And he was like, 'Yeah, but no one's

really done it before.' And then I started thinking about it properly. One of my favourite shows is *The Office*, because it uses that mockumentary style. Sam pointed out that reality TV was starting to change and that audiences were starting to understand how it worked.

Sam
Yes, people knew that these shows aren't fully real, that there's set-ups and scripts and all that, but they were still watching. So the sitcom was going to be a massive piss-take of the industry and find the funny in the less glamorous side of what people think is fame.

Pete
You know, like travelling through the night in a knackered Ford Fiesta just to get to Newcastle so someone can shout 'cunt' at you on a sticky nightclub stage.

Sam
Or opening a kebab shop and stinking of onions when you've got a first date straight after. Or watching someone who's been in the game five minutes shoot past you because they've got a better jawline, and they're doing brand deals with L'Oréal, while you're pushing fucking John West tuna.

Pete
So that was the set-up. It was a scripted parody, based on the shit we'd been through. Never was it our intention to actually act in it, but then the production company told us they wanted us to do it.

Sam
We were like, 'We can't fucking act.' And they said, 'You can't play yourself?' I mean ... it's basically method acting, right? So we gave it a go.

Pete
I genuinely don't think they could've found anyone worse to play Sam than Sam. Acting's not his forte. He had said to me beforehand, 'I just don't know if I can do it.' And I went, 'But you are him. Just be you.' Bless him, he tried so hard, he was Daniel Day-Lewis. He wasn't. Though I wasn't much better.

Sam
When the pilot was in the can – as they say in the telly world – the production company sent it out everywhere, to all the channels. Without wanting to sound cocky, we were actually pretty confident someone would snap it up, because regardless of whether we could act or not, the idea was the best thing we've ever come up with. And it wasn't just us who were confident about it. The production company were too.

Pete
But as it turned out, no fucker wanted it. Wasn't the right time, apparently. They didn't believe in it. I don't think we were seen as credible or popular enough. So the sitcom went nowhere.

Sam
I was gutted, I have to admit. And I think I took the rejection personally.

Pete
I wasn't surprised by the reaction, but I was disappointed. Because honestly, I still think it's the best thing we've ever done. But you never know, it might be something we may start thinking about again. So keep your eyes peeled – you never know what might be around the corner.

I BEGGED HIM TO DO A PILOT, PROMISING HIM THAT IF IT WAS SHIT, WE'D NEVER DO IT AGAIN

Pete

So the sitcom was a no-go, and Sam was devastated about it. But as you're aware, you can't keep that Duracell Bunny down for long. Before I knew it, he'd come up with the idea of *Staying Relevant*, the podcast you all know and love. He'd been banging on about doing a podcast for a while, while I had never listened to one. I couldn't think of anything worse. Listening to some self-important tosser waffle on about their self-indulgent shit? No thanks.

But, as is always the way with Sam, he persuaded me. Forced me, really.

Sam

It took me months to get Pete to do it. I was calling his agent every single day for, like, half a year. No joke. I was like, 'Please, I promise you, this will work! It'll be good for us. It'll keep us relevant, put us out there so that the right people still know we exist.' As much as I loved the idea, I knew that it was also a very important tool to help us establish ourselves as a duo. At this point in time, podcasts were a thing, but nowhere near as popular as they are now.

Pete

Yeah, everyone and their fucking mum has one these days. I have to admit, I wasn't bothered about podcasts. It sounded like a lot of hard work, and for what?

Sam

Well, Pete is lucky that he's got me.

Pete

How do you work that out?

Sam

Because I don't come up with ideas just for me – I come up with ideas with you in mind. Because I know what you're capable of. All I need to do is get him sat down and *bam* – he's off. That's my thing. I like to think I bring out the best in him.

Pete

Fair. If it wasn't for him, I'd probably still be out boozing with mates, watching serial killer docs! Instead, I spend most of my waking hours dressed up in Lycra with Sam hanging out the back of me! Jesus, what has my life become?

Sam

Anyway, I begged him to do a pilot, promising him that if it was shit, we'd never do it again. As it was the first one, it was one of the most budget things you've ever seen.

Pete

We had one bit of paper with a couple of bullet points on it. And that was it. Bare bones.

Sam

But wouldn't you know, it ended up being one of the best episodes we've ever done! It was just us chatting about how terrible and chaotic the podcast was. Well, Pete was saying that. I was trying to hype it up and act like it was this huge deal, which to me it was. I was sat there, all excited, and he was like, 'You're reading off an A4 sheet with nothing on it,' and 'You've messed up the intro,' and 'No one's gonna listen to this shit.' Just ripping it to pieces the whole time. But when we put it out there, people loved it. They loved the way we sparred with each other. They loved the chemistry we had, which they'd kind of seen on *Celebs Go Dating*. It went to number one in the charts. Number one! We never thought that would happen. But it did. And that's where it all started.

Pete
And so *Staying Relevant* was born. The idea was simple – just tell some of the ridiculous stories we've lived through. We used to laugh our tits off about the mad shit we've done over the years, so why not share that with everyone else?

Sam
To begin with, we teamed up with a production company. They brought in other people to write stuff for us. It started out all right.

Pete
But then it started to drift a bit because it wasn't us. You could feel it. It just didn't sound like us any more.

Sam
Nevertheless, the podcast was doing well. So well, in fact, that our agents suggested we do a tour.

Pete
A tour? I thought, Who the fuck's gonna pay to see two talentless tits chatting shit on stage? I genuinely didn't think we'd sell any tickets. I'd never been to a podcast show, so didn't know what to expect. But I didn't put up a fight and went along with the idea. And that opened another can of worms.

Before we hit the road, everyone was telling us we had to get writers to help with the show. But I was like, 'No, I'm doing it.' I wasn't a writer, but who better was there to put words in our mouths than me? Sam, supportive as ever, threw me right under the bus.

Sam

Yeah, sorry, mate. I kept telling anyone who'd listen, 'Pete's writing it. So if it's shit...'

Pete

Cheers, mate.

Sam

Well, we were new to the game, and I really wanted the tour to be great! I reckoned we should just get as much help as we could. But Pete wasn't having any of it.

Pete

I stuck to my guns. Everyone told me not to, but I thought, Nah, I'm doing it. And guess what? The initial dates sold out, so we had to add more pretty much immediately. Then the second dates sold out. Honestly, what a moment for us – it all became very real.

Sam

The podcast just took off. I loved every minute of it, and I was buzzing that so many people were tuning in and had bought in to what we were about. I always knew it would work and was so pleased it was doing well.

Pete

But eventually, it started to stagnate a bit. We got to a point where we wanted to do it our way. By then, we understood ourselves a bit more – and we'd started to enjoy all the behind-the-scenes stuff. So we thought: screw it. Let's go it alone. I was the one really pushing for it. I think after that first tour, I had more confidence. I thought, We can do this. Why not?

Sam

We were really grateful for the start we had, but it was

time to go it alone. We've been in the game long enough to know how it all works. And honestly, there's no better way of learning how to produce something than watching it happen around you. As we said, we've always been matey with the behind-the-scenes people and you pick up a lot from them.

Pete

And it paid off. In the first month of doing it ourselves, we went from strength to strength. And this was before Sam did the jungle. We doubled our listeners within a few months. And we didn't change much, we were just doing it our way. To this day, I can't tell you exactly why there was such a big shift. But there was. And it just felt more us. Because it *was* us.

Sam

Then we set up the production company, pulled together a great team, and we planned to grow things slowly ... but it's gone mental.

Pete

Not that you're all that involved in the day-to-day, waltzing into the studio at lunchtime! Honestly, if it weren't for the success of the podcast and the doors it opened, would we have even got offered *Strictly* or *I'm a Celeb*? And would we have done as well on those shows without our listeners voting for us?

Sam

Going it alone was a risk. And it was the best decision we ever made.

Pete

That's when I really started to enjoy it. I've never liked being told what to do – I've always done it my way. But there's a period of time when you go along with stuff, because you're learning. And then one day, you realise your career can actually be yours. Taking ownership was the best thing we ever did.

At Home with Sam and Pete

Pete
We're super close and are in each other's pockets practically 24/7, so *Staying Relevant* listeners have constantly asked why, oh why, don't we live together?

Sam
Good question! Why don't I just move in with you? Can you imagine us shacked up together ...

Pete
No thanks. Don't want to. Actually, we don't need to imagine it. We've done it when we went on *The Circle*. And what a nightmare that was! If you ask Sam, he'll say it was the best thing ever. If you ask me, I'd say: never again. Probably one of the worst weeks of my life.

Sam
I thought it was brilliant. I learned a lot. For instance, Pete shits with the door closed.

Pete
Obviously.

Sam
I actually shit with the door *open*. Pete doesn't like talking in the bathroom. He's a silent assassin when he's relaxing. Doesn't want to chat. No chinwag. Just sits in silence.

He's a bit of a carer, though. He'll cook potato smileys, spaghetti hoops ...

Pete

And I'll do the tidying up too, and clear away all of Sam's toys at the end of the day.

Sam

There were a *lot* of toys. And he's a sucker for a game of Connect 4. He's really good, too.

Pete

We played, what, like six hundred games? We had nothing else to do.

Sam

He also likes a fag.

Pete

What I learnt from my week under the same roof as Sam was that he has a very strange habit. Now, you know kids have a blankie that they like to hang on to? Well, Sam uses his penis in the same way.

Sam

So true.

Pete

Just to make him feel safe. If we're sitting there with the telly on or he's chilling out, he'll have his hands down his pants, holding onto his cock.

Sam

I genuinely think it's an ADHD thing. I always have to fiddle with something.

Pete

Also, he *has* to lie across the sofa, stretched out like a cat.

Sam
I do love a sofa sprawl. But do you know what's interesting? Pete doesn't like to lie down across sofas. He sits upright.

Pete
Like I'm waiting for a fucking bus.

Sam
He does. He will sit with his back straight. Literally. Won't even lean back on the sofa. It's like he's in church. I try and rest my head on his lap – not happening.

Pete
At dinner, I'd cook.

Sam
Remember when I wet-willied you? You got so pissed off.

Pete
Not that anyone needs to know, but a wet willy is where you lick your finger and stick it in someone's ear.

Sam
Classic. And he got fucking furious.

Pete
So, I'd make dinner, serve it at a certain time, and then sometimes after dinner or even during it, Sam would get distracted and wander off, pick up a toy like a ball and start playing catch – mid-meal. Then at the end of dinner, I'd do the dishes while he drove a remote-controlled car into my ankles. It was practically every night.

Sam
Like clockwork.

Pete
It was semi-funny the first night. By night three, I was done.

Sam
And when we went to bed ...

Pete
In separate rooms.

Sam
We'd say goodnight to each other and ...

Pete
You see, when I went to bed, he didn't like to be alone. So he would go to bed too. As far as I was concerned, we were both in our rooms, and that's it. We're done talking. But no. Not Sam. He carried on jabbering.

Sam
And there were no doors in the bedrooms, which was great. Every time we'd go to bed, I'd get up, poke my head into his room. And he'd be like, 'I know you're there.'

Pete
So Sam would say, 'Pete? You still awake?' And I'd be like, 'Well, obviously, I'm in fucking bed, aren't I? I'm trying to sleep.' Then in the mornings, I was normally up before the alarm. And then Sam would be up when the alarm rang.

Sam
But I wore an eye mask to block out the light.

Pete
I don't get why people need an eye mask. Just close your eyes.

Sam
Nah, mate, I need full-blown darkness.

Pete
But is there not full-blown darkness when you close your eyes?

Sam
You see, eyelids aren't thick enough. Go on, close your eyes now.

Pete
That's fucking ridiculous. Sam is one of those people that if there's a gadget to help something, he'll have it. I'm quite basic. If you want to go to sleep, close your fucking eyes. So, bottom line for anyone asking if Sam and I could ever live together: the answer is never.

Sam
Never say never.

Pete
I'd say never, unless one of us needs a carer.

Sam
I invited Pete to stay at mine once, when he was between flats.

Pete
I chose a hotel instead.

Sam
But I went around telling everyone that he had been evicted and was living in my attic.

Pete
Yeah, this pack of lies went on for three months. People were like, 'Sam, you're so kind.'

Sam
I'm just that generous.

Ain't that the fucking truth!

Sam: my bad habits
I've got a lot that irritate Pete. One of my biggest is the 'burp and blow'. I get really gassy. I have to let it out. And he hates bodily functions. So that would definitely be one. Another would be my touching. I'm very touchy-feely. He'd say that's my worst trait.

is. Just get your hands off me!

Pete's bad habits (by Sam)
He's very final. if he doesn't like something, he's just, 'I don't like it.' And you're like, 'No, just hear me out.' And he's like, 'No, I don't like it.' You have to break him down – it takes hours.

My Weirdest Pete Dream

I've had two dreams where Pete's been my guardian angel. I was flying – I like to call it astral projecting, because I believe in that stuff. So, I was flying through the universe, and Pete was beside me. Then we saw this really dark hole next to a tree, and I said, 'I'm going to go in there.' And Pete said, 'No, you can't – it's not good. That's where the bad things are.' Then I woke up – and it was Pete who woke me up.

And then I had a dream where we were being chased by a T-rex – which happens more often than you'd think. About twice a year I get chased by a dinosaur. Every time, someone's in the dream, but most recently, Pete was there too. To start with, he was running away from it. Then he stopped and actually tried to knock the dinosaur out. And then I woke up!

What the fuck?

What are you fucking on?

Your mind is scarier than I already thought

16

Doing It Ourselves

THE INDUSTRY IS FULL OF DOORS AND IT'S ALL ABOUT PICKING THE RIGHT ONES

Pete
Podcasts are different to telly. They're more natural. No watershed, no channel bosses. You just do what you want. The truth is – and Sam would back me on this – regardless of *I'm a Celeb* or *Strictly*, to date the podcast is the best thing we've ever done in our careers. No question.
  Along with my *Man Made* podcast. And my dog show.

Sam
No need to thank me, Pete.

Pete
As much as it fucking pains me to say it, you were . . .

Sam
What was I?

Pete
. . . right. It really is the thing we're most proud of. Because *we* made it ourselves. So now I can say this is my job. Which

is nice, because for the first time since I started out in this industry, it actually feels like I'm doing something real. Like proper hard graft. It's like I've found this little pocket of the industry where I actually know what I'm doing. And all of it was born out of two fucking idiots chatting absolute shit.

Sam

I had a feeling it was going to do well, but I never thought that within a year of taking over the pod we'd be where we are now. In the early days, we didn't know shit about setting up a production company or running a podcast.

Pete

Bottom line: if you don't try, you'll never find out if you can do something. I've failed at a million things. I've had businesses fall flat. But if you spend your life doing what everyone else wants you to do, you'll only ever get so far. It's been a mad journey. From meeting on *Celebs Go Dating* to, however many years later, headlining the fucking O2. With our own business. Our own show. Done on our own terms.

If someone had told me the day I met Sam that we'd still be mates all these years later, I'd have said, 'I'll kill him before then.' No chance. Let alone running a business together. But here we are. And we never planned any of it.

Sam

Well, I knew we'd get here. I just did. I had faith in us.

Pete

Jesus, maybe you really are a mad genius that pulled it all together without me realising. It's the only time anyone could ever call you a genius, but I think on this occasion you rubbed both of your brain cells together and thought, We can do something.

Sam

This industry is full of doors. And it's all about picking the right ones. Fame's weird like that. It can end at any second. You could go viral overnight – or fall off a cliff just as quick. There's no stability. None. Same with popularity. But notoriety? That's different. That's the only thing that lasts. You can be notorious for being good – or notorious for being a twat – but either way, people remember you. You're either popular or you're not. And fame? Fame just dances somewhere between 'on the way up' and 'has-been'. All it takes is one blink, and you're a has-been. We're one blink away.

STAYING RELEVANT IS TOUGH. FIRST, YOU'VE GOT TO GET THERE. THEN YOU'VE GOT TO STAY THERE

Pete

At the time of writing this book, Sam has landed loads of work after his stint in the jungle, while my time on *Strictly* has opened me up to different audiences. I've also presented a TV show, *For Dogs' Sake* on U&W, which has been another of my proudest moments so far. I'm actually an associate producer on it too, if you can believe that! So does that mean Sam and I are finally relevant? Is the podcast now null and void?

Sam

Of course not. Becoming relevant can happen at any moment. But the hard part is maintaining it. You could win the lottery, but you might spunk it all in six months. So then what? How do you grow it? How do you keep hold of it? That's the bit no one talks about.

Pete

Staying relevant is tough. First, you've got to get there.

Then you've got to *stay* there. And honestly? I'm still not entirely sure we're there. I don't know when we first became 'relevant'. I genuinely don't. You can only do your best with whatever's in front of you. But the thing is, what's in front of you in this game? It constantly changes. I don't know what 'relevant' even is. I mean, yeah, you can define it. But what does it mean to me?

Sam

You getting asked to do *Strictly* – that was mental, because they don't normally ask reality TV people on that show.

Read more about this in Part 5, folks

Mark Wright and Jamie Laing did it – and Tasha was in my year, you tit!

Pete

I never thought I'd end up doing *Strictly*. It's one of those shows, same as the jungle, that everyone wants to do – apart from me. Don't get me wrong, that's not me slagging it off. I know how successful it is and how much the country loves it. But I've never been much of a TV watcher, so it's never been something that was on my bucket list. I mean, I hate the idea of dancing. As you may have seen, I can't do it. A fucking stick insect has more rhythm than I do. To me, it was just another job, albeit a job that I absolutely loved.

Sam

But look at how things were changing for us. We were becoming more relevant because we were being taken seriously. When I landed my gig on *Love Island: Aftersun*, it was the first time I actually felt like I'd made it. Like I'd gone legit. I remember thinking, Me? That's great.

I'd been doing loads of Instagram stories about the show, so I like to think it was my digital content that got me the gig. Mike Spencer, a lovely guy who's the creative director now, got in touch and said, 'We'd love you to do the podcast and come on as a returning guest.' And I thought, That's pretty cool.

In turn, I got a bit of kudos for that and became part of the ITV family!

Then later that same year, I was asked to do *I'm a Celeb*, which I fucking jumped at. And when I came back from that I felt like I was ready for my next challenge – to host stuff. Finally! I've had some amazing opportunities come my way, like my presenting spots on *This Morning*. The guys there have been so good to me and made me feel very welcome. I feel lucky. I am still yet to host something myself, but the future is feeling bright.

WHEN PEOPLE START KEEPING YOU AT ARM'S LENGTH, THAT'S BECAUSE THEY KNOW YOU'VE LEVELLED UP

Sam

The big turning point was the podcast. When that started doing really well, people began looking at us differently – like, 'Hang on, these guys actually have something.' And again when we started our own production company, people started going, 'Oh, this is actually good,' 'Oh, they're getting like a million listeners a month,' 'Oh, they're headlining the O2.'

Suddenly, there were big companies treating us like we were their rival – which I find fucking hilarious. But that's when you know you're doing something right. And the best part is: *we've* done it. Like Pete, I'm super proud of it. I've always wanted to run a production company. It's such a beautiful thing, knowing that Pete and I have achieved so much and are doing well. We know what works. We're at a point where we can sit in a meeting with a big company and push back and tell them we don't agree with something. I'd never have done that before. But now I can, and that's a cool feeling. We're really proud of what we've achieved, especially with the production company.

Pete
I actually think we're really fucking lucky. Because we've had the ups and the downs and really grafted.

Sam
We've had a slow rise and, because of that, we've learned a lot. And as time goes by, we've got noticed. We've been nominated for a variety of podcast awards over the years, but have always come away empty-handed.

Pete
Even when dopey-drawers was convinced we were going to win.

Sam
But then, in June 2025, something amazing happened.

Pete
Yes, something did!

Sam
We got nominated for a TRIC award. And guess what?

Pete
I have a feeling our readers will remember.

Sam
We won! We bloody won, beating legends like Peter Crouch, Davina McCall and the *Shagged. Married. Annoyed* team.

Pete
Well, I already knew we'd won, because Producer Pippa and I had been told earlier that evening. But we didn't let on to Sam, 'cos with his big gob he'd go round and tell everyone. In the end, when we got announced Sam jumped up on

stage like the Duracell Bunny, waving his fucking camera around while I did a speech.

Sam
Your speech was awesome! What was it you said again?

Pete
Something like, 'We are a couple of absolute wallies, but we started this two or three years ago, and I'm blessed to have won something with my best mate.'

Sam
I started doing a bit of a speech, but then I totally dried up, so I shut my mouth and let you take over. That was such an awesome day, and what an amazing honour. We never expected to win, based on our previous disappointments. So we made the most of it, and we turned up to the event in a stretch limo with Josh and Producer Pippa in the back. When I got out it was like the Oscars, with the waiting crowds asking for autographs. Even Pippa and Josh were asked to sign some autographs.

Pete
Yeah, I saw. But awards are one thing – what about when you went to Buckingham Palace to meet the King for the King's Trust event you were involved in?

Sam
I know, I still can't believe I was there.

Pete
And I still can't believe you called the King 'mate'. He must have thought you were a right knob!

Sam

Oh, don't. I'm still so embarrassed.

Pete

You're lucky they didn't chuck you in the Tower of London.

Sam

I was flustered and hadn't got my bearings.

Pete

And you were flustered because?

Sam

Because I was late.

Pete

Late to meet the King.

Sam

Well, I'd been here doing the pod and had to get across London to Buck Palace as fast as I could, but ended up getting there a bit late. If that wasn't bad enough, I realised I didn't have my invitation with me, so I had to haggle with this super-serious guardsman who clearly didn't want to entertain me. Eventually I made it in and got taken to where everyone was, and was shoved into a queue next to someone who was already chatting to the King. Then the next thing I know, King Charles steps up and sticks out his hand, the softest hand I have ever felt. Anyway, the next thing I know, I'm saying the words, 'You all right, mate?'

Pete

Prick! Even I know you can't address the King like that.

Sam
He caught me off guard. And that was the first thing that came in to my head. The funny thing is, I'd been practising what to say, over and over.

Pete
And you'd been practising your bow.

Sam
Well, I wanted it to be perfect, 'cos it's not every day you get invited to Buckingham fucking Palace to meet the bloody King. Anyway, the minute the words fell out of my mouth I could see his aide flash me a very unimpressed look, and I went, 'Oh, shit.'

Pete
You actually swore at the King?

Sam
Yes, I swore at our ruler.

Pete
You should be ashamed of yourself.

Sam
Oh, I am. So then I tried to make the best of it and nodded at him and said, 'Sir!'

Pete
You said what?

Sam
I know. And then it got worse and I said OUT LOUD, 'God, you're not even a sir,' before mumbling, 'Mate … Sir … Your Majesty …'

Pete
He must have wondered, Who the fuck is this silly twat?

Sam
Probably, but by the end of it he was laughing. He was actually really nice. He's a good guy. I feel like we bonded, and seriously, the work he has done with the Prince's Trust and now the King's Trust is just amazing.

17

Behind the Scenes of *Staying Relevant*

Producer Pippa, Digital Josh and TV Ted reveal what life is like in the Staying Relevant *office.*

Pete
As regular listeners know, *Staying Relevant* isn't just about Sam and me.

Sam
Well, it is – we're in the illustration!

Pete
As the pod has evolved, we've curated a team of fuckwits – Producer Pippa, Digital Josh and TV Ted, and a few other behind-the-scenes types – who have become inexplicably popular with listeners. Tossers, the lot of them, but they're our tossers.

Sam
To be serious for a minute...

Pete
You what?

Sam
I can be serious sometimes.

Pete
Go on, prove it.

Sam
Our team is the lifeblood of the entire thing. When we started, it was just me and Pete doing a very basic podcast.

Pippa is the best, and the heart of the entire operation. She came in at twenty-five – young – and she's now one of the most respected podcast producers in the entire industry. That's all down to her. Her tenacity is unmatched. She's a joy to be around. I nicked her from my radio show. I saw the talent instantly. I said to Pete, 'We need her.'

Ted has been working with us for eight or nine years. Certainly with me. He's like our little brother. Actually, not so little any more. He'll be involved in everything we do – TV shows, production company stuff. He's one of our must-haves.

And Josh – he's one of the nicest, loveliest blokes. He just *gets things done*. He's the quietest of the three, but he's just as valuable. You know those quiet guys where, if they're not there, you really notice? He's that guy. We literally picked people who are like us. It's like they're characters in a comedy sketch – but the difference is, they're unbelievable at their jobs.

Pete
Anyway, because we've reached that stage of the book

where we're sick of the sound of our own voices, we thought we'd let them have their say about life at *Staying Relevant* Towers. Appraisals, if you like.

Office Appraisals

SR Team

Hi guys, it's Team Relevant speaking. Sam's gone off gaming with Badger 68, while Pete's gone out for a fag, so it's our chance to let you know what really goes on behind the scenes. We'll keep it snappy.

Appraisal topic: personality traits

- **Sam's high-energy and excitable**

Pippa: It gets said all the time – he's like an excitable golden labrador. You'll walk into a room and Sam's already bouncing off the walls, full of energy, full of enthusiasm. He never sits still. He's really affectionate, genuinely interested in what you're doing, but in a way that's almost chaotic.

- **Pete's cynical and dry**

Pippa: He's the perfect antidote to Sam's golden labrador energy. Sam sees rainbows, Pete sees the clouds behind them.

- **Sam's warm and affectionate**

Pippa: He'll always hug you but will ask 'Can I give you a hug?' first, which is funny, because by that point he's basically already hugging you.

- **Pete's guarded but loyal**

Pippa: You have to earn Pete's trust. He doesn't just let you in, you have to prove yourself first. But once you do, he'd move mountains for you. He's fiercely loyal.

- **Sam constantly seeks validation**

Pippa: Every day, he'll ask whether his outfit looks good, if his hair looks good, if he should dye his beard.

He asks what shoes he should wear, what jacket. He needs constant affirmation. Even if you're in a serious meeting, he'll say, 'What do you think of this top?'

- **Pete's blunt but not nasty**

Josh: Pete's blunt. He'll tell you what he thinks, straight to your face, but it's not offensive. It's never nasty.

- **Sam can be endearingly blunt**

Pippa: He'll walk in and immediately say to someone, 'Rough night?' or 'You look like absolute shit today.' But it's never cruel. He says it with a huge smile, and you can't help but laugh.

- **Pete's an old-fashioned gentleman**

Pippa: Pete's proper old school. Handshakes, direct eye contact. He insists on it. He has proper manners, proper respect.

- **Sam lives in his own bubble**

Ted: It's genuinely like *The Truman Show* with Sam. Only the people and things in his direct line of sight exist.

Pippa: We'll be stuck in traffic and Sam will say, 'Where is everyone going? What are all these people doing?' I think sometimes he forgets people are living their own lives.

- **Pete is soft once you get through**

Pippa: Once Pete lets you in, he's one of the most generous people you'll ever meet. He'd do anything for you.

Appraisal topic: work habits

- **Sam has zero inbox management**

Pippa: Sam's *Staying Relevant* email account had over a thousand unread emails. I had to physically open his inbox and link it to his phone. And then he rang up two days later, saying, 'Pip, how do I stop these email notifications? They're so annoying.'

- **Pete always knows what to do**

Pippa: Whenever we don't know the answer to something, we all say, 'Just ask Pete.'

- **Sam has little awareness of company operations**

Pippa: For all he knows, the company could have made zero money. He has no clue how it works, no idea about the finances. He literally once said, 'Wait, how much money do we actually make from this?'

- **Sam's casual and disruptive**

Ted: He'll randomly decide today's the day he takes his shirt off. No warning, just shirt off. Or he's dyed his beard without telling anyone and turns up purple.

You guys are always encouraging me to do it

- **Pete always looks smart**

Pippa: He carries a briefcase with him wherever he goes, and takes real pride in his office attire – he has a new jacket every week.

- **Sam focuses mainly on socials**

Pippa: Sam's main update in a Monday meeting is, 'The socials are doing good.' He'll genuinely contribute nothing else, but will say it with so much pride.

If I eat your food, it means I love you. Share food, share ideas, share thoughts. Slightly unorthodox, maybe, but it works

- **Pete loves structure**

Pippa: Pete is organised, decisive, loves structure, loves process. He's discovered emails now and he's obsessed.

- **Sam's a lunch thief**

Pippa: He'll stroll over, look in your Tupperware and go, 'What's this?' before eating half of it. Doesn't even ask if he can have some. And if it's nice, he'll finish it. If it's not, he'll tell you it's shit. And still finish it.

- **Pete's all about work–life balance**

Pippa: He's always the first to suggest a pub trip as soon as the clock hits 5.30 p.m. (sometimes earlier).

Appraisal topic: on set and recording days

• Sam has hype-man attitude

Josh: Before the mics go on, he's pacing the studio saying, 'Right, team, let's have a good game! Big energy! Let's smash it!' like it's the World Cup Final.

• Sam is a bonus content enthusiast

Ted: On Sam's good days, he will beg to film TikToks after recording – 'Let's do more, what else can we do?' – while Pete looks like he's about to throw himself out the window.

• Sam's job interview technique

Pippa: During one interview, he got up mid-call, stood there in just his pants and microwaved a full roast dinner ready meal while the poor candidate kept talking. He was burping loudly during another one.

He asked one candidate what star sign they were, then did a full astrological analysis even though he doesn't know anything about star signs.

After each call, Sam would say, 'I'm sure we'll be seeing you again,' basically promising them the job, even if we weren't hiring them.

• Pete won't sugarcoat anything

Ted: He'll look at you and say, 'What the fuck have you come as?' if he doesn't like your outfit.

Appraisal topic: team environment

• Fun but chaotic

Pippa: Working with Sam and Pete is like being the mum of triplets, even though there's only two of them. Every day is a full-on circus, but you're laughing the whole time.

- **It's non-hierarchical**

Josh: There's no 'celebrities and staff' vibe. Pete and Sam treat you as equals – when Pete's not having a go at me! We are a group of people trying to make each other laugh.

- **They cultivate genuine office friendships**

Josh: Sam and Pete want to know about your family. They invite your partners to events. You're part of the family.

- **Extremely loyal**

Pippa: If I was in trouble at 2 a.m., Pete and Sam would be the first people I'd call. And they'd come without hesitation.

Ted on meeting Sam and Pete

I met Sam in 2019, because I was filming with Ryan and Sam's sister Louise. First interaction: he just came over, super high energy, talking about how he wanted to start a YouTube channel. He basically poached me from Ryan within three months.

Pete, I met about two years later, when we put him into a human-sized balloon in Sam's garden. That was the first time I'd ever seen Pete – and probably the angriest I've ever seen him too.

For context: we put Pete in the balloon and he nearly suffocated. And honestly, that kind of set the tone. For a long time, Pete and I never really had proper conversations. About two years ago we had a breakthrough. We were leaving a shoot and he didn't know how to say goodbye. He kind of went to hug me but wasn't sure. That was the first time I saw the softer side of Pete.

Digital Josh on meeting Sam and Pete

The first time I met Sam was in my job interview. I'd already spoken to Pippa and Ted, then they brought me on to a second call with Sam. He turned up not wearing any trousers – but then neither was I. I was on holiday and wearing trunks; he was just at home.

Sam's really welcoming. The first time I met him in person, he gave me a massive hug. We bonded over being Chelsea fans, so I felt quite at home.

Then Pete walks in. He wasn't on any of the interviews, so I was already a bit nervous because he hadn't met me. The first thing he said to me was, 'Look at this tall cunt,' and turned around and walked off.

Pete's great, but you have to prove yourself to him. Even now, almost a year later, he still kind of rips into me, but I really like him. I actually have more in common with Pete than Sam – like, we're into the same music, we grew up at the same time, similar experiences.

Summary: Pete and Sam as bosses

- Sam turns up just before the podcast starts. He eats everyone's lunch, hugs everyone (with consent) and talks mainly about how his outfit looks.
- Pete would protect you with his life. He's the most loyal, generous guy once you've proved yourself.

Nights out and social life

- Pete is extremely generous and insists on paying for everything. I've never had to buy a drink when I'm out with him. The one time I did, when we went to the pub and I bought him a Guinness, he was mortified. He was like, 'How are you buying me a drink? What the

hell?' And I thought, I probably owe you about thirty thousand drinks.
- On nights out, Pete assigns everyone a number. Before we leave, he'll call out, 'One ... two ...' and wait for everyone to shout their number in turn, just to make sure no one's left behind. Pete's properly like the dad of the group. He'll order all the cars, make sure everyone's got a ride, and then he'll text you when you get home: 'Are you home safe?' Every single time.
- Sam is the first to say how big the night is gonna be and how we all better 'buckle in', but orders tequila shots too early and is always the first to go home in an Uber. He reckons the next night will be the big one, but we are all still waiting!
- Sam loves a team talk and a motivational speech on a night out, and of course a group hug for good measure.

Josh's story: *Strictly* car alarm disaster

When Pete was doing *Strictly*, Sam wanted us to film some stupid TikTok with him during training. I got to Elstree Studios first. I called Sam and Pippa to say, 'Where are you guys?' and they were like, 'We're stuck in traffic, about forty-five minutes away.'

It was absolutely pissing down with rain. I was waiting outside – still no sign of Pippa and Sam. When they finally arrived, Sam was like, 'Let's just go in.' I said, 'Maybe we shouldn't, they're still filming,' but Sam was like, 'Nah, it's fine.'

He bangs the door open and bursts in wearing a pair of fake boobs, shouting, 'What's up?' Everyone turned around. Pete was dancing with his partner Jowita, they were filming his *Strictly* training for a VT and we completely disrupted it. Pete was livid and ordered us back to the car, but then Sam's car alarm went off. Continuously. Just blaring. It got picked up on all the BBC cameras. They were filming *Hamlet* next door, and the alarm ruined that as well.

Pete was texting us, like, 'If that's your fucking car, turn it off now.' Sam didn't care, he just blasted Justin Bieber out of the speakers and was rapping with the windows down.

I was sitting there thinking, This is amazing ... but I'm definitely getting fired.

Pippa on fan encounters

Every single time someone recognises Sam, he acts like it's the first time. He's so thrilled. After a fan takes a photo, he'll walk away and say, 'Oh my God – as if they wanted a photo with me!'

After Sam won *I'm a Celeb*, everything changed overnight. Before, maybe once a week someone would stop us in the street. After the jungle, you couldn't go five metres without someone asking for a photo.

Pete never says no. He'll always stop, shake hands, have a chat, pose for a photo. He's very polite, very old-school about it. But you can tell he finds it weird. It's like, 'Why do they want this?' He doesn't quite get it.

When I went with Pete to the *Strictly* tour, we went into All Bar One for dinner. Within seconds, it was like a Pete Wicks meet-and-greet.

Podcast highlights

The Olive and Rose segments, where Pete and Sam talk about their hypothetical daughters. They have become a big part of the podcast now. Olive is Pete's daughter, Rose is Sam's, and they put them in these hilarious situations, puberty, dating, sending them to uni – it's become a real narrative.

Shag, Marry, Kill is so popular with listeners, and Sam and Pete take it really seriously. Like, genuinely debate it for ages.

The 'Pete doesn't exist' thing has become massive. Whenever Pete does anything normal, like getting the Tube or going to Sainsbury's, the internet loses it. People message saying, 'I want to see Pete doing his laundry or taking the bins out.' They can't believe he does normal things.

Anything where Pete reacts to something ridiculous, like Jellycats or those Labubu keyrings, goes viral. He just combusts at how stupid the world is now.

A day in the life of the *Staying Relevant* office

9 a.m.: Pete implemented a rule that everyone is meant to arrive at the studio for 9 a.m. Josh is always there a bit before – he's an early bird. Everyone else kind of arrives around nine. We have a nice little quiet hour as a team without Pete and Sam. Calm before the storm. We go through the plan, clips, bits we want to film. It's quite a nice hour.

10 a.m.: Pete usually turns up around ten, swearing and muttering under his breath, angry about something minor like coffee spilled, traffic, anything. His classic opening line is, 'Three hours, I spent in the car!' or 'Left my house at half past five this morning.' He's normally wearing some kind of co-ord, like a matching set or tracksuit, and you'll smell the cloud of cologne before he even arrives. He sits down, opens his laptop with a big sigh and says something like, 'I'm working till nine tonight,' or 'Gotta go to Leeds after this filming.' He carries this little Louis Vuitton briefcase everywhere, glued to him like a limb.

12 p.m.: Sam rolls in around midday, for the recording of the podcast. He's like, 'Morning, team!', even though we've all been there for three hours by that point. He'll walk in, headlock a couple of us, drink someone's tea, tell everyone, 'The socials are doing good,' and start asking for compliments about his look. Week on week, there's something new to comment on. Maybe his mullet's longer, maybe he's dyed his beard a different colour – whatever it is, it's dramatic.

2 p.m.: We try to get them into the studio. Pete's usually fine, but Sam will need to faff: 'Oh, I need a fag break,' or 'I need to check my hair.' You have to coax them in. Sam will usually start with a pep talk, he'll shout, 'Let's have a good game, everyone!' Pete usually just groans and tells him to get on with it. We record the main episode first. Then they'll take a fag break outside, Pete with his LV briefcase tucked under his arm. Then we usually try to film extra social bits, like TikTok trends. Pete protests a lot; Sam loves it.

4.30 p.m.: After recording, we go back to the office. Sam usually tries to leave immediately and will make up some kind of dramatic excuse.

Pete, on the other hand, will stay for another hour, working through bullet points and plans, but if you try to ask him something directly, like 'Have you made a decision on this?' he'll just grumble 'No.' The time after recording is usually much less productive. We might end up talking about what shows we're watching, or just laughing about nonsense.

Part 4

What Comes with Relevance

18

The Dark Art of Social Media

We live in modern times, where TV is just one way to get noticed. Thanks to Sam and his wild imagination, we've become social media legends.

Pete
As we know from earlier chapters, Sam is the social media whiz. I can't be arsed with any of it. Why? Because I'm a grown man pushing forty. I've got Insta, but I try not to use it. I post stuff because I get forced to. It's kind of part of my job. But I don't live my life on it. Well, I try not to. These days, everyone's sharing every aspect of their lives – or worse, posting clips they reckon are comedy. (I know, pot calling kettle ...) But in my defence, it's work. I'm only all over TikTok, dancing around like a prick, because of stupid-drawers and his madcap ideas. I've never even watched a clip of our posts because ... well, I don't fucking want to. I've had to mute Sam just so I won't see them. I can't watch another video of him pretending to be a *Harry Potter* DJ in his sister's living room.

Sam
That's when I'm living my best life.

Pete
Exactly, and that's just sad. Call me old-fashioned, but I can't fucking stand how people can't function without their phone. One of the many things that pisses me off about Sam – and there are many – is that you'll be mid-conversation with him, and suddenly you lose him. He vanishes into a twenty-minute TikTok rabbit hole.

'What are you doing?' I'll ask.
'I'm just looking at a giraffe on TikTok.'
'What?'
And then it moves on to someone dancing like a giraffe.
And then it moves on again.

Whereas it's not really for me. That said, all this Tik Tok crap has become a massive source of income for us. Not that it stops me from loathing every single minute of it. I'm happy to take the money, don't get me wrong, but that doesn't mean I don't see it for what it is: total bollocks.

So, while Sam bangs on about how social media changed his life and made him a fortune, let me be the adult here, the lone voice of reason. Because the problem now is, people think social media will make them famous.

Sam
What I love is that this industry's becoming more childlike, with all the TikTok dances, avatars and so on, and I find it hilarious to mix that with people like Pete, who are the total opposite. He reacts in such a fun way. Like on the podcast, I love the moments when Pete's confronted by stuff like the Jellycats, and the AI Sam and Pete babies.

Pete
Well, I still don't understand that Jellycat bollocks. And

don't get me started on those freaky kids! Are you sure they weren't real?

Sam
I love the way you are so genuinely bewildered by it all. Hilarious. You were like a seventy-year-old man. I find it so funny, genuinely fucking funny. I'd love to see Pete do role-play, like *Dungeons & Dragons*. I'd love to see him build a character and story. All of these ideas involve Pete being the star. I just want to be the co-pilot on that journey, taking him into these situations and letting him shine.

Pete
Oh shut up, you tosser. We are in this shit together.

Sam
That was always the idea: for Pete to be the star. Any show idea I've ever had, including the podcast, has always been tailored around Pete. When you put him in unfamiliar situations, that's when you get the best version of him. I saw it before he even realised. And it's been amazing to watch his development in the entertainment space. I think it's made people really bond with him. It's made him feel more real, like, yes, he's a macho man, but also a guy having fun with his less-macho mate. I think it's helped people see a side of Pete they wouldn't normally get to see.

Now, what's great is that he's doing stuff that merges both sides. Like his dog show – that's done so well. It's a true passion project for him. And now people know him well enough to embrace the real Pete.

I can't stress enough how cool it is to hang out with your best friend and just talk. Every week with him is a fun experience. That's my happy place. If I was ever down and he asked what he could do to cheer me up, I'd say, 'Let's film a stupid video.' That's what makes me happy.

Sam's Three Favourite TikTok Moments

1. Inflatable animals. There have been so many funny ones to whittle down, but I do love our TikToks where Pete has to dress up as an inflatable animal. I'm usually the inflatable cow. He's the inflatable pig.
2. Fart spray. My favourite one I've ever done is the fart spray one. I got him in the car, said we were filming a singalong TikTok. But secretly I was spraying fart spray while we were recording. He kept saying, 'What's that smell?' but didn't clock for half an hour. He just thought I was *actually* farting. It was one of the funniest things I've ever done.
3. Spider-Man. He absolutely hated doing that one. Anything too touchy-feely, he hates. So I had to persuade him to do it by pleading with him to do it for the people, to which he said, 'I don't give a shit about the people.' But he does, and he did it. And that's why the people *love* him.

I JUMPED ON HIS BACK, SLAPPED HIS ARSE AND HE LAUNCHED ME ONTO THE SOFA

Sam
Celebs Go Dating Digital was our first job together, doing digital hosting for the show. We'd do watch-alongs with other contestants, round at my place, interview them, chat, react to the episode. A bit like *Gogglebox*. It was the first time we actually worked together as a duo.

Pete
I'd only go round to his because I was contractually obliged.

Sam
I remember the first TikTok we did, Pete was a horse.

Pete
A fucking horse!

Sam
He had really long hair, and it looked like a horse's tail. I jumped on his back, slapped his arse, and he got up and launched me onto the sofa. No one had seen anything like it before – everyone was still taking social media really seriously at that point. No one had seen a joke like that, just pure, chaotic silliness.

Pete
Nor had anyone seen a reaction like mine before.

Sam
No one had seen Pete get annoyed in that way, because it had always been through the lens of a TV show. And suddenly here's this big, tattooed man's man getting his arse slapped and flipping out on TikTok. He throws me off

and goes, 'What are you doing?' And everyone watching was like, 'This is fucking hilarious!' That's when I realised, Holy shit, he hates this stuff. I didn't fully get it before that moment. I thought he was just playing along. But nope. He really didn't like it. And I thought, This is gonna be brilliant.

It was like *An Idiot Abroad*, putting someone who hates something through the exact thing they hate doing. That became the formula. I started making him do dances in the garden, wearing ridiculous costumes. When we did the first video, I told Pete he had to practise the dance before we filmed it. So what did I do? I set up a second camera in my garden and filmed Pete learning the dance without him knowing, then cut down the footage into a montage of him getting it wrong and getting fucking angry. I put it out and got something like ten thousand comments. Pete was this anomaly, this grumpy, no-bullshit bloke being forced into doing TikTok dances. He despised it. And he despised me.

Pete
Wasn't hard!

Sam
When he came over to do *Celebs Go Dating Digital*, I'd always make him do one TikTok. Then, when they started doing really well, things got interesting. These days, people say to me all the time, 'Well, he must know by now ... You've been doing this for, like, years. It's got to be a set-up.' And I go, 'This is where you're wrong.' Because it's morphed into something even better. Back then, I had to force him to do it when he came round.

Pete
And now my agents are booking me in, because they know it works. The numbers are good. The audience loves it.

Sam

To start with, I had to be a clever secret squirrel. I used to book some time on a Friday with his agent. Friday was content day at mine. It got to the point where he once got an Addison Lee from his house, thinking it was a branded deal.

Pete

He told them not to tell me what it was for. Just said it was a job. So I get picked up in a car, thinking I'm off to a proper shoot – you get used to not knowing where you're going sometimes, you just get told it's work. The car pulls up outside Sam's house and I'm thinking, All right, maybe we're filming at Sam's. I walk in and I go, 'What are we doing here?' And he goes ...

Sam

I've booked you for the day.

Pete

So I literally went, 'Are you joking?' And then I called my team and said, 'Well, invoice him, then.' He thought I was joking. But the fuck I was. I made sure he got charged full rate. I told my manager, 'Bill the twat.' He literally booked me to come round and film a pointless TikTok dance. *They didn't!*

And it doesn't stop there. When we are on a job, the call sheet will say the wrap time will be 3 p.m. So I'm thinking, great, early finish. But then Sam pipes up, 'Yeah, you're booked till four. We've got time now to do a little dance...' Turns out the little tosser's spoken to my management and added an hour on to my working day, so I can't go home, and I get roped into more bollocks instead!

Sam

But it makes me happy.

Pete

I'm glad someone is! I don't think I've ever looked at one of our TikToks and laughed. Not once. But Sam? He'll sit there watching them back, crying with laughter, even clips from two years ago, because he cannot believe he's managed to get me to do it.

Sam

You're comedy gold, mate. You just don't realise how funny you are!

Pete

With anyone else, I'd say no. Absolutely not. But with Sam, it's like he's testing the boundaries. It's turned into a game for him: 'How far can I push Pete?'

That's when you know your life's fucked – when Sam Thompson is your bully. I mean, fuck me. That's how far we've fallen. I think he's probably the one in control, to be honest. The manipulative little fucker.

He gets me to do all sorts, and I cave and do them. It's funny, because I never ask him to do anything. Ever. Except one thing: fuck off. That's all I've ever asked of him. And it's the one thing he won't do. The only thing I've ever wanted from him – to be left alone. And it's the one thing he can't manage.

Sam

Do you remember the time your hair got stuck in the leaf blower? I almost killed you.

Pete

I had really long hair at the time, and it got stuck in the leaf blower. I'm not even joking, it ripped a patch out of my head. That was the beginning of the receding hairline. I'm blaming Sam.

Sam

Can I tell you the panic I had? That was the first time one of these stupid things had gone seriously wrong. I put him in one of those giant balloons that go all the way up to your head and the balloon completely suctioned around him – he was just sitting there, totally stuck.

Pete

It was like I was trapped in a used condom, lying in his garden, getting choked and shouting 'CUNT!'

Sam

I'm panicking, looking at him getting strangled by the thing. I need to get air in there so he can breathe, I thought. So I grab the leaf blower to force air in, and then his hair gets caught in the fan. He's going, 'What's going on? Sam, what have you done?' I've never seen a man angrier than Pete in that balloon.

You know, we should do that again some time. Remind me to order another one off Amazon.

SOCIAL MEDIA IS BRILLIANT FOR SOME THINGS AND ABSOLUTELY TOXIC FOR OTHERS

Pete

Okay, so these days I have to deal with social media, but I will admit, I don't really understand what I'm doing and what it's for. Don't forget I come from a time when we had to do proper graft to make money. No one my age went to school thinking, You know what I want to do when I grow up? I want to post outfits of the day. Or, I want to unbox shit for the rest of my life. Sorry, what? That's your job? You want to open gifted crap from brands and call that a career? Fucking blows my mind. But if it works for someone, fair play. Who am I to piss on their parade? But I still can't get

The Dark Ages (the eighties)

my head around why anyone should give a fuck about what some arsehole they've never met is having for their lunch.

Sam
Can't you see the benefits of that?

Pete
Benefits? What benefits? What am I getting from watching someone chop up a salad?

Sam
Well, you might pick up some handy tips from what they eat in a day.

Pete
Tips? I know how to fucking eat. I've been doing it all my life.

Sam
Yeah, but they may have had a body transformation.

Pete
Then post a recipe. I don't need to see some twat in a swanky flat telling me how much they love avocado on toast sprinkled with chilli flakes. Why do I care what you stick in your gob? Just eat the fucker. Don't talk about it, don't film it, just live your real life.

Social media's changed everything. It's brilliant for some things and absolutely toxic for others. It's created a bunch of morons who've rejected the real world and now only exist online. Maybe that's harsh, but it feels that way.

INFLUENCERS MUST WORRY THAT SOMEONE YOUNGER, FUNNIER OR WITH BETTER TITS WILL TAKE THEIR PLACE

Pete
These days, doing silly dances and lip-synching to telly clips is a job. Not a hobby, a fucking job. From the outside, being an influencer looks easy: take a pic of your dinner, get free shit, lie on a beach. And often, that's bang on.

Sam
But being a social media bod is also hard work. It's not as easy as you'd think. You've gotta keep the content coming, you gotta stay relevant, just like us. 'Cos if you slow down, lose your momentum, you risk losing everything. So you can't afford to get lazy. You've always got to be 'on', otherwise someone younger, funnier or with better tits will take your place. You've got to stay relevant.

Pete
Fair enough, I get that. I just don't understand why people tune in to watch them do the most mundane things. I can sort of understand the TikTokers who do a silly dance, but the ones who just share their everyday existence? What's that about? I don't understand what's so exciting about a Boots bag! Why do people at home care? Don't they have lives of their own? Their own Boots bags? I guess people want to see inside someone's life, inside their homes. It's a bit weird for me, but then I'm probably not the target market.

Sam
Is it any different from how we started out? Maybe this is just the modern version of reality shows like *MiC* and *TOWIE*. You only ever see the beautiful, filtered version of their lives. You don't see them having a shit or a wank.

Pete
Unless you're signed up to OnlyFans.

I STUCK PETE IN A BEAR COSTUME AND RODE HIM THROUGH FULHAM

Pete
If there's one thing that I can say about Sam, it's that he is inventive. Sam's the one who comes up with all the stupid ideas and mad campaigns. Half the time I think he does it 'cos it gives him a buzz. But if it gets clicks, it's cash. It's easy money.

Sam
Brands come to us, ask for a funny video to fit their campaign, and I have to admit I'm like a kid with a pot of crayons. Last year, Coors asked us to do a campaign with them. Their TV ad had a bloke riding a bear through the mountains so, naturally, I stuck Pete in a bear costume and rode him through Fulham.

Pete
I wish he was joking. That actually happened. But the thing is, we know we're taking the piss. We're not doing it seriously. It's daft, but that's the point. And it's still work.

Sam
We're not pretending to be cool, we're leaning in to the fact we're both twats.

Pete
Our audience gets it. They're in on the joke. We all know it's ridiculous. What I hate is when you get some celeb doing an ad, like, 'I wear this brand every day. It's the only place I shop.' And you just sit there thinking, No you don't. You're saying that 'cos they're paying you. Whereas we're like, 'Look, I've been told to say I wear this jumper every day, so

here I am, saying it ...' But then I'll go, 'It is actually quite nice.' And people see that and go, 'Fair play.'

But I'll give Sam his due, if it wasn't for him and his love of social media, I wouldn't be living the life I lead now.

WHEN YOU'RE GOING THROUGH THIS WEIRD JOURNEY OF BULLSHIT, DOING IT TOGETHER IS BETTER THAN DOING IT ALONE

Pete
From the outset, Sam had a plan for what he wanted us to do.

Sam
I predicted – more like hoped – that we'd be like Ant and Dec.

Pete
More like Dick and Dom. Luckily, we just liked doing stuff together. Without sounding soppy, he's actually made things better. I find him funny because he's weird. I think he finds me funny just because I'm also fucking weird. And when you're going through this weird journey of bullshit, doing it together is better than doing it alone.

But then, when I'm lying awake at night, sometimes I wonder if it's too late to get a restraining order as sometimes he crosses the line.

Sam
What do you mean?

Pete
You always tell me that you find me fascinating, which is weird as you've known me for so long now.

Sam
But I do.

Pete

Which is just creepy. And very strange. He'll say weird stuff like, 'I could just watch you.' Even with mundane things – 'You pouring me a glass of water fascinates me, the way you do it' – and I'm like, 'I don't get what you mean.'

He always wants to record everything I'm doing because he just finds it baffling. People can't imagine me just being at home. I think people must think I go into some sort of coma when I'm not recording the podcast or on TV.

Sam

See, the world is baffled by you, Pete. It's not just me.

Pete

Listeners send in stuff like, 'Imagine Pete putting on his socks.' But why would you want to? 'Imagine Pete doing a food shop.' 'Imagine Pete washing his car.' And I'm like, 'These are just normal things ... Why can no one imagine me doing them? Who or what do you think I am?'

Sam

Well, I'm wondering right now how you wipe your arse! Back to front? Or front to back?

Pete

Well, you're not going to find out unless I shove your head down the bog! Sam's always been like that. If I go to the bar and buy a drink, he'll say, 'It's just so weird when you do things.' I'm like, What? It's all really odd.

Sam

I love to watch Pete doing life ... it's utterly hilarious. That's where all the dances and other stuff for TikTok come from. I just think, People need to see this. Because in some ways, Pete is this mysterious being that none of us really know an awful lot about. I find the really boring, normal stuff he does incredibly fascinating. I think his life should be narrated by David Attenborough.

Pete
And I'm like, I just don't get any of that.

Sam
Because no one really knows anything about you.

Pete
Well, if people ask, I might tell them.

Sam
You don't really tell anyone anything.

Pete
Because I don't like to share too much. Which brings me to...

19

Fandom

When you go on telly, it doesn't matter who you are or what you've done, people start looking at you differently. Like you're not normal any more, like you're some kind of alien or you've got two heads. Just the fact that you're on TV makes some people think you're more special than you actually are. But where would we be without the fans, the very people who have helped us become the men we are today?

Pete
I'll be honest, at first it was a bit of an ego boost. You get the attention, people are nice, it's flattering. But that wears off pretty quick. Then it just becomes weird. You start noticing little things, like the stares, the whispering, and it all gets a bit much. Makes you feel on edge, like you've always got to be 'on'.

And this has made me more of a hermit. I only go to places I know, places I like. My circle's smaller. Life's changed – not loads, but enough to notice. I know not to go to the shops during the day now because it'd take me the whole day to get from one end of the street to the other. Don't get me wrong, everyone's nice and that, but it makes living your real life hard. Not that I'm complaining.

Now Sam, he's a different story. That prick absolutely loves it. He loves the attention!

Sam
I mean, I adore it. There was a time right after I won *I'm a Celeb* when I got mobbed in a shop – it was such a cool feeling. People were coming up, talking about my ADHD and all just smiling. Saying things like, 'I want a Sam Thompson hug!' It was so nice. You see, I'm an energy person. If there's a crowd with amazing energy, I love it and I'm buzzing. Whereas Pete would be like, 'Nah, this is a bit much.' He's not that kind of guy.

Pete
You're not wrong. If a bunch of randoms tried to give me a fucking Sam hug, I'd be out of there faster than Usain Bolt.

Sam
Well, I think it's a lovely thing to do. I can really feel people. Not physically, but emotionally. I can feel people's energy a lot. There are people who've followed my journey – and Pete's too – from really early on, and they're so welcoming and invested it makes me feel like I owe them something.

Pete
Like what?

Sam
I don't know, but I genuinely think I *do* owe them something – because I'm allowed to live this dream life *because* of them. And the reason they allow me to do it is because they're really nice people. I just feel like I'm in debt to people for making me feel so loved.

I had a hard start to the year. And every time I've gone

through personal things, people online have wished me well and supported me. I've realised that I'm very much an online person. I really seek online communities.

As cringey as it sounds, I know I have come from a really privileged background and went to a good school. But I squandered all of it. I didn't have any real prospects, academically. I failed most of my exams. I'm not clever in that way. But so many of my dreams have come true because of the connection I've formed with people I've never actually met.

Pete

See, kids, you too can start out a total uneducated twat and end up being adored by the public by just gobbling down a kangaroo cock! Seriously, though, mate, it's great you've found your way. I've never seen you look so happy and fulfilled.

Sam

Aww, thanks mate, that means the world to me.

NIGEL FARAGE GOT PAPPED WITH SAM FOR CLOUT

Pete

It's not just fans who want to have a picture with you. Celebs do too, only they tend to get a snap for clout.

As you know, Sam was in the jungle with Nigel Farage, who, for a short minute, people thought might actually win, 'cos 'he came across all right on the show'. In the end, he finished third, and no sooner was he back in the real world than he reverted to his usual ways. While we were waiting for Sam to come out, he said to me, 'Who'd have thought being an idiot could help you to win?' I think he was being kind of jokey, but I thought, You don't know me well enough to joke about my best mate, and snapped back, 'Better than being a cunt.' He laughed.

Anyway, fast forward a couple of months and Sam and I were at an awards ceremony. Sam's not very observant, and was lost in his own world anyway, but I spotted Farage and a couple of his geezers are heading in our direction. I could see that one of the guys was filming him, so I was pretty wary of what was going on. Nigel rocks up to us and bellows, 'Hey Sam, lovely to see you!' Sam stands up, gives him a big hug, as he does, and the guy's filming the whole thing. Sam goes, 'Pete, Pete, get in on this.' I went, 'Absolutely not,' and walked away.

Next day, the headline was 'Sam and Nigel Farage Discuss Politics'. Okay, so I can't exactly prove that this was Nigel's plan, but I reckon he just wanted to be relevant and to be seen with the King of the Jungle, the popular guy of the moment. I mean, who wouldn't? Politicians are just as keen to stay relevant with the public, so it makes perfect sense.

20

When Being a Celebrity Changes Other People's Lives

CRYING MUMS TELL SAM HE'S THEIR HERO

Pete
After I wrote *Never Enough*, in which I looked back on the tough times I'd been through in my life, I was inundated with messages from people asking for help or guidance. Now, don't get me wrong, I'm chuffed that I have a platform that enables me to touch people's lives and help them navigate their own tough times – that really is an honour and it makes me feel like I did the right thing in opening up so much. But sometimes I can't help but feel this immense pressure, especially when they tell me, 'You're my last hope. I don't know what to do. Please reply or I'm going to kill myself.' I can't reply to everyone, of course, but I also know I'm probably not the person who should be offering advice, which is why I always signpost mental health charities and helplines.

Sam
Pete and I do a lot of funny stuff, which is great – making

people laugh is what we try to do. But when you start using your platform for something a bit more serious, it can be overwhelming.

Pete
Sam's a massive role model now, especially for people with ADHD and autism after he got diagnosed. I've been with him when mums come over in tears: 'You've helped my son. You're his hero. I saw you in the jungle...'

Sam
I mean, what can I say? I feel so proud that I can help people in some way. I don't know how, but I guess just seeing someone like me living with ADHD and autism can make people feel less isolated. A couple of years ago I signed up as an ambassador for ADHD UK, and am intent on changing perceptions of those with ADHD, trying to encourage conversation around the topic.

After I left the jungle, so many children and adults contacted me to say I've helped change their minds on how they view ADHD and autism. My goal was to try to reach as many people as I possibly could, especially young people, and show there is some kind of magic in being neurodiverse. I'm not denying there are some very real challenges, but with the right support, I really believe it can be a superpower, it can be a blessing, and we can achieve all of our dreams.

Pete
It's lovely. But it's also big. It's a lot of responsibility, being the poster boy for ADHD. Because then people want to be around you, talk to you, share their stories. And you can't do that with everyone. There's pressure there.

Sam
What are you the poster boy for?

Pete

Just ... John West tuna. But yeah, when you put yourself out there, people do feel like they are connected with you in some way. After I spoke about the work I did for animal welfare charities to make sure dogs are safe, I got inundated with messages asking, 'Can you help with this dog?' Then after *Never Enough*, people clearly felt like they could get stuff off their chests.

I ain't gonna lie. A lot of it was heavy. But I feel really proud that I might have helped people feel comfortable enough to open up and let things out. That is so important. Keeping stuff bottled up doesn't help anyone in the long run. But as I said earlier, I'm just a 'TV personality'. I'm not a counsellor or an expert. I wouldn't know where to begin to solve people's problems. I can barely deal with my own. But I am more than happy to help share people's stories about life challenges, like I do on my other podcast, *Man Made*, that asks the question, What makes a good man, and more importantly a good person?

Sam

That's why we are so happy to help with charity stuff. In summer 2025, I embarked on the maddest adventure I've ever done, the Match Ball Mission, where I ran, walked, cycled and cried my way from Stamford Bridge to Old Trafford, covering more than 260 miles in five days, to raise money for UNICEF as part of Soccer Aid. I'm not gonna lie, I thought it was going to kill me.

Even though I'd spent four months training, it turned out to be tougher than I ever expected. On the first day, I tore my calf 40k into the first marathon. The pain was excruciating. It felt like I'd been shot. I had to hobble the last 2k. I panicked, because there was so much riding on me finishing the mission. When I got to the first stop, the physio Gary Lewin told me I might not be able to run for three weeks. I was devastated. I thought I had let everyone down. The people who'd asked me to take on this challenge, the people who were supporting me and the kids I was hoping to help with the money raised. I thought I was failing. I was convinced they'd picked the wrong person.

Pete
Back in the *Staying Relevant* office, we were getting updates. We were so proud to see you start off strong on the Monday morning – you were off! Then three hours later we heard something had happened.

Sam
It was touch and go, and I was advised to do the next jaunt by bike. Every pedal push hurt, but it was a pain I could deal with. I was so relieved that I was back on the road.

But what got me through was the support of people like Ben Shephard, Chris Hughes, my future brother-in-law Ryan, Josh Patterson and Tony Bellew surprising me on the route. The power of friendship really kept me going. And the support from the public. I mean, when I saw you, Pete, I thought I'd reached the end.

Pete
When I saw you coming towards me, I'd never felt prouder. All week we were wondering when we should meet you on the journey. Should we be there near the start, the end or in the middle?

Sam
When I saw you, I basically fell into you. That meant a lot, man. Having the whole team there – it lifted me. I've never felt anything like it.

Pete

I don't think I've ever seen you so emotional. And I've seen you cry when someone tells you your new hair colour suits you.

Sam

It's funny, at that point in the challenge I felt so low, and yet so high. So to see you, to hear you, meant everything. I knew you'd turn up along the way, but I thought it'd be at the end. So when I did see you, on the third day, I was at my lowest!

Pete

I didn't know what to say to you. I didn't know how you were going be feeling. And as much as we take the piss out of each other, I decided it wasn't the best time to poke fun at your teeth or thinning barnet! But we did cheer you up with some hilarious banners.

Sam

I needed that. By the time I'd got to you, all I could think about was letting everyone down. That all the people who had taken on challenges before me – like the amazing achievements of Jamie Laing, Spencer Matthews, Josh Patterson – had completed them. I was worried that I would be the one to fail. But then when I saw you and you gave me that pep talk, it changed everything. It put so much joy in my heart! After that, I headed off along the road to Liverpool.

That journey was so hard, but I don't think there was a better time for me to be alone, pushing myself. It was one of the most mentally freeing times I've ever had. We rode and ran for so long, and the pain was so excruciating that I needed to channel something to get me through, and I think I left a lot of what I'd gone through that year out on the road. I didn't speak to Tracy, my cycling mentor, for an hour and a half, and twenty minutes into me not speaking she said, 'Whatever you're channelling now, you need to keep doing it.' And I just rode like I had never ridden before, crying. When I got to Liverpool, I fell off my bike and burst into tears again. I had never felt so emotionally drained. But also so at peace.

Pete
Well, it was your way of processing some things that were hanging around in your mind.

Sam
It was a weight that I had been holding on to for a lot of that year, and I finally managed to shake it off. And then Tony Bellew turned up to take me across the Mersey!

Pete
Which was one of the most beautiful – and also hilarious – things I've ever seen.

Sam
As I've said before, you guys, and the public, got me through the agony I was experiencing, and when I reached the finish line, I felt so proud. Not because I had finished the challenge, but because so much money [2 million] had been raised for charity. And I knew where that money was going first hand, because earlier in the year I had visited Guatemala, to see how the funds would be used.

I'd never been there before. It's a country where only 4 per cent of children have access to early education services, and more than half experience chronic malnutrition. It was very humbling. I met a girl called Dany whose communication and motor skills weren't very good. But six months later, she had completely changed. She was coming over to me, taking my hand. I found it so emotional. To see someone so young and innocent be given a chance to live their best life meant so much to me.

My experience visiting Guatemala was a real wake-up call. It made me realise how privileged I am. How lucky I am to have the life I lead. Stuff like that reminds you that all this striving to stay relevant in the showbiz world is pretty stupid in some ways. But then, trying to make it like Pete and I have has presented us with ways to make other people's lives better in the process. By lending our names and time to help. Getting involved in that challenge was my way of showing people that there's more to me than being a labrador and, more importantly, raising a shitload of money for children who need it.

Pete
Well, you should be proud of yourself.

Sam
Aww, mate, thank you! And you know what? I am!

Pete
Not just because of completing the challenge and the fuckload of money you raised, but simply because of the person you are.

Sam
Hang on a minute, where's this going?

Pete
You know, you are genuine, authentic and a truly lovely person. That is rare, and something to be very proud of in itself.

Sam

Hang on, where's the real Pete?

Pete

It's not about ticking boxes or reaching goals. You should be proud because you're an incredible human being, full stop. You did what you did for an amazing cause, but also, importantly, for yourself. To feel something deeper about yourself, to feel that pride.

Sam

Come on, where's the punchline?

Pete

No punchline. This is me being straight up! I know you wanted to prove to yourself that you are more than just the labrador, but I've known that about you since the day we met.

Sam

Mate, I think I'm gonna well up.

Pete

Well, it's not like I haven't said stuff like this before.

Sam

I know, but I love to hear you say it.

Pete

I mean it from the bottom of my heart. That said, I'd also be willing to pay a few thousand quid to get you to cut that fucking mullet off!

Sam

Ooh, I'm tempted. But while I think about it ... do you

remember that time you got your cock and balls out on the telly?

Pete
I certainly fucking do! For *The Real Full Monty* Christmas special. I really enjoyed doing that show – the cast and crew were great to work with. I think I was the only person who wasn't too bothered about stripping off, probably because a lot of people had already seen me naked.

Sam
Once seen, never forgotten!

Pete
I've not heard that before! Anyway, I didn't mind getting my kit off; it was the fucking dancing that bothered me. This was way before I did *Strictly*. So you can imagine how awkward I was, thrusting my hips and waggling my cock about on stage in front of a live audience that included my poor fucking mum! It was a great show to be part of and personal too, as my uncle had had cancer, and I'd had a cancer scare myself when I was younger. It thankfully turned out to be okay, but I remember worrying about it so much that I was too scared to go and get it seen to. In the end, I did get it checked out because all I could think about was what if I left it too long? Where would that leave my mum?

Sam
That's good to hear. And I bet you made more men examine their balls more often than they did before. I'm always here if you need me to help check yours.

Pete
No, Sam. Not ever.

21

The Reality of Reality

The life of a reality star can be glamorous – but a lot of the time it's not. You can't piss in peace and there's always someone only too eager to tell you what they think of you.

ALL MOST PEOPLE ON *TOWIE* WANTED TO DO WAS TO OPEN A SHOP IN ESSEX

Sam
Reality TV has changed so much, especially since the days when Pete and I were on our shows. The innocence of it has kind of disappeared.

Pete
People no longer go on these shows as themselves, so it's not reality any more. In the beginning it was basically a social experiment: normal people doing normal things. That's what *TOWIE* was. That's what *Made in Chelsea* was. Now we see more and more people going on these shows who want to land a brand deal with the likes of Pretty Little Thing or who want to be a presenter. Back in our day, you wouldn't go on *TOWIE* thinking, Next stop: *I'm a Celeb, Strictly, Celebs Go Dating*. Back then,

all most people on *TOWIE* wanted to do was to open a shop in Essex. No one went into it thinking, I want to be a presenter, or I want to be famous. It was more like, Can I make a few quid and open a shop? But then, when the opportunities that came with the job started rolling in, the cast began to change.

Sam
All of sudden, people realised these shows could be a stepping stone.

Pete
And that if you do enough of those shows, you get to be seen as more than just Pete from *TOWIE*. You become Pete the TV personality, or whatever. Once I'd done a few other shows, that's when it started to feel like I had found myself a proper career.

Even though I' been hanging around for years, I still can't get my head around the idea of a TV personality being an actual job. It ain't something you'd tell your careers teacher you'd want to do.

Sam
Maybe in this day and age.

Pete
But it's a legit job. These days I can say I present and produce documentaries and podcasts, but I used to hate being called 'Pete Wicks, TV personality'. What does that even mean? It's bollocks, if you ask me. Try filling out a car insurance form: 'What's your occupation?' What are you supposed to put? It's hard to type 'professional cunt' – doesn't go down well with insurers. But seriously, how is it a job when I'm just being myself? Then again, look at how much the world's changed. Once upon a time, playing

computer games was just what losers like Sam with no girlfriends did as a hobby.

Sam
Oi, I love gaming.

Pete
My point exactly! And which is why you like to spend most of your time at home alone, playing with your eleven-year-old mates in Japan. But now it's a career. These hobbies have become careers. That's just how it is now. But I still can't get my head around it.

The irony doesn't escape me that Sam and I make a living in pretty much the same way. I'm not complaining, but I'm old school, so none of it really makes sense to me.

Sam
That's 'cos you were born so long ago! Get with the programme, grandpa!

ONE MINUTE THEY'RE GOING TO CRACK AMERICA, THE NEXT THEY'RE DOING A LOCAL RADIO SHOW

Pete
What I did start to notice along the way was that no matter how much fame or notoriety people would get from being on the kind of programmes Sam and I were, there was a serious danger of losing it. When I joined *TOWIE*, there were some people who had moved on with big career plans that just sort of ... fizzled out. But that's just how it goes. There's *always* someone new. Someone fresher. Better looking. More current.

Sam

Stuff like that inspired the whole idea of *Staying Relevant* – how do we keep going when we're not the shiny new toys any more?

I THINK SAM'S STRUGGLED GOING FROM 'THAT BLOKE OFF *MADE IN CHELSEA*' TO KING OF THE JUNGLE

Pete

Sam and I have been doing this job for over a decade, and the question I keep asking myself is: do I want to be on screen for ever? Probably not. So part of setting up these companies and projects is my way of planning for the future.

I think Sam's starting to agree. He always wanted to be the face, to be front and centre, but now I see a shift in him. I think he's struggled with the growth – going from 'that bloke off *Made in Chelsea*' to Sam Thompson: King of the Jungle, Sam Thompson TV, Sam Thompson everyone-knows-your-name. And I think that level of attention has hit him harder than he expected.

Sam

Yes, things changed so much after the jungle. The attention became more intense. Now, don't get me wrong, I love people coming up to me, I absolutely live for it, but the intensity of it came as a surprise and it took me a while to get used to it.

Pete

I went into this business blind, without wanting it. But Sam chased it – then got it – and maybe now it's not what he thought it was gonna be.

Sam

Oh no, it is. It is *everything* I thought it would be. The good parts, anyway. I love doing the work. I love making TikToks, doing the podcast, the live shows, doing the radio and telly stuff. Chatting to the fans. I love being creative. It's just the extra stuff I could do without.

Pete

Now there's this pressure – everyone wants to know what he's doing, every second. And when he's going through tough times in his personal life, like his recent break-up, that pressure is unbearable.

Sam

People feel like they deserve to know every personal detail, just because we're on the TV. They seem to forget what you're going through. Imagine experiencing some personal trauma and people are pointing at you, laughing at you, trying to find out what's going on. And all you want to do is hide away and find a way to heal in private.

In fairness, I did put my relationships on social media. I knew what I was doing and people become invested in what we got up to. But then, when something bad happens, can't I have a moment to deal with it? Of course, I understand people will want to know what's going on, but when you're feeling sad, the last thing you want is people making you feel even worse.

Pete

But it's like that because we've come from reality TV, where we've shared a lot of ourselves with the public, including about our relationships. Most people get to go to work, come home and have a home life. Ours – home, work, private life – it's all just one big, exposed life that everyone can fucking comment on.

I CAN'T GO FOR DINNER WITH A WOMAN WITHOUT SOMEONE ASSUMING WE'RE MORE THAN JUST FRIENDS

Pete

Your relationships, where you go, who you're with – I can't go for dinner with a woman without someone assuming we're more than just friends. Even my *mum* has been my 'mystery woman'. I mean, we're a close family, but not that close.

Sam

And remember that time we were at Marvin's fortieth birthday? We were papped with your radio boss, who was described in the press as your 'mystery woman'. It was mad!

Pete

It's shit because it starts affecting the people around you. And that's what I struggle with. I'm okay with people having opinions about me – fine. I chose this. And most of the time I can laugh at it all. But I didn't choose it for them.

A Day in the Life of Pete

We've talked about it loads on the podcast, but now we finally get to find out exactly what Pete does when he's not living his life as a superstar.

Sam
So come on then mate, satisfy the nation's curiosity and reveal all about what you really get up to when we don't see you.

Pete
Really? Is this still a thing? I mean, what do people think I do? Sleep on a fucking cloud with angels playing a harp next to me? Shit on a golden throne?

Sam
Er, yes! That's exactly what we think. So come on, then: what's the first thing you do in the morning?

Pete
As soon as I wake up, I get straight out of bed. No snoozing.

Sam
Really? I press snooze about four times before I get up.

Pete
Nah, not me. I'm not a snoozer. First thing I do is switch on the coffee machine and make a very strong coffee. Usually a triple espresso. Then I go outside and smoke three cigarettes. I won't speak to anyone or even look at my phone until I've had that coffee and those three fags. It's like a sacred ritual. Then I chuck on a tracksuit, take the dogs out for a walk, come back, feed them and then finally have a shower.

Sam

And do you do your teeth in the shower?

Pete

No, always at the sink. I don't get people who brush their teeth in the shower.

Sam

Yeah, I guess that's just weird.

Pete

After that, I put on my little patches under my eyes.

Sam

He loves an eye patch, does Pete.

Pete

Listen, I'm not getting any younger. I've got puffy eyes. I need to de-puff before I can do anything else, otherwise I look like I've been dug up.

Sam

And you keep them in the fridge, right?

Pete

Yeah, they live in the fridge. But just before I shower, I chuck them in the freezer so they're extra cold. It's a proper de-puff situation. After all that, I'm set for the day. Ready to rumble.

Breakfast

Sam

What about breakfast? Do you eat anything?

Pete
Not usually. I'm not a breakfast guy. But if I know I've got a really busy day and I might not eat for a while, I'll make some porridge.

Sam
What do you put in it?

Pete
Nothing. I literally have plain porridge.

Sam
That is classic Pete. Just plain porridge. Nothing in it at all.

Pete
It's like eating sand. I don't even enjoy it. I just do it when I have to.

Morning toilet habits

Sam
We haven't talked about morning shits. So, coffee and three fags – no way you're not having one.

Pete
I don't. I shit at 4 p.m. every day. Like clockwork. Just one big dump. Done.

Sam
I'll have two in the morning, and I won't have even left the house.

Pete
Nah, mate. I'm efficient. One and done.

Sam

I'm like five a day. Constantly clearing out.

Pete

That can't be good.

Sam

Don't know. But my sphincter is always in motion. Honestly, I've got piles.

Pete

You need cream for that.

Clothing and wardrobe

Sam

Let's talk clothes. Is your wardrobe like Simon Cowell's, all matching and perfectly ironed?

Pete

Sort of. I mean, I'm thirty-seven and I still take my washing to my mum once a week. She irons everything. Then I bring it home and hang it up. But I don't decide what I'm wearing until the morning. Might try on a few bits, depending on what I'm doing that day. Nothing is colour coordinated, but my clothes are in three different rooms.

Sam

Do you know what's in each room?

Pete

It's organised chaos. I know where everything is, no one else would.

Sam
Do you know how to iron?

Pete
I know how to steam. I can iron if needs be, unless it's a shirt. If it's a smart shirt, it's difficult to iron. I'm very particular about how they look. It must be starched correctly. You can't have creases on things like that. Which is the opposite to you, really. You love a crease.

Sam
I do love a crease.

Pete
Quite often Sam looks like he's ironed his clothes with a brick.

Sam
I haven't ironed anything for about four years.

Pete
So who does all the washing?

Sam
Well, I have someone who comes in.

Pete
His au pair does the washing.

Sam
I don't have an au pair. Anyway, I do feel like clothes uncrease. I don't have an ironing board, so couldn't iron even if I wanted to.

Pete
So how do you iron your clothes?

Sam
That's the thing, I don't iron my clothes. You just wear them and your body heat actually de-creases them.

Pete
What? So what you're saying is you're a sort of part-time podcaster, part-time iron?

Sam
Genuinely, if you wear your clothes for long enough, they un-crease because of your body temperature.

Pete
But they're creased when you put them on. What happens if you have a morning meeting?

Sam
I'd just turn up and go, 'Look, don't worry, I'll send you a photo in three hours and my clothes won't be creased.'

Pete
But you have to wear un-ironed clothes for three hours.

Sam
Yeah, but if you just explain to them that you're in the process of un-creasing ...

Pete
'I'm sorry, I'm in the process of un-creasing!'

Sam
Exactly. You'd say, 'Unfortunately, you've caught me at the stage where I'm still a little bit creased.'

Pete
It's fucking ridiculous. I remember when we were on tour last year, Sam turned up on the first night in a pair of horrendous skinny jeans, high-top trainers and a creased T-shirt. And I said, 'So what are you wearing tonight?' And he said, 'Well, this.' So I told him, 'You look like you just got out of bed.' And he was like, 'Oh, I didn't realise we had to wear something different.' Mate, you're on stage in front of three thousand people.

Sam
I need to be comfortable, man. I need to be in my mufties.

Pete
But to be fair – hang on, your what?

Sam
You've never heard mufties? Home clothes. Casual wear. Comes from boarding school, I think.

Pete
I don't even understand the concept of home clothes. People ask, 'What do you wear when you get home?' And I say, 'Whatever I had on that day!' Like today, when I go home tonight I will literally stay in this until I go to bed.

Sam
No, no, no. I change at least twice a day. The moment I walk through the door – straight into trackies. It's the best. Sometimes shorts.

Pete

He's always in shorts. Basketball shorts.

Sam

I love basketball shorts. Or I like to mix and match. Sometimes, I will feel like a no-sock day. I just walk around the house barefoot.

Evening routine

Sam

So what happens when you get home after a long day of being Showbiz Pete?

Pete

First thing? I try to forget all about you! Then I'll make myself another triple espresso and have three fags. Then I say hello to the dogs, take them out for a walk, come back in, put on some music and sit. I just sit. For like an hour. Staring at the wall.

Sam

You don't watch telly?

Pete

Only if I'm in the mood. Usually, I only put the TV on to fall asleep. I need noise to sleep – something going on in the background.

Sam

So if you're home alone, you don't read, or sit there and think?

Pete

Nah, I don't really think. I just blank out in some meditative vegetable state.

Dinner and cooking

Sam
What about dinner? What do you make?

Pete
Depends on the day. Sometimes, if I'm really busy, I'll forget to eat. But usually something simple – stir fry, bit of pasta. Very easy. I don't have to cook for anyone else because ... well, I'm sort of sad and lonely. So it's just cooking for me.

Sam
And you're not a microwave person?

Pete
Nope. Don't even have a microwave.

Sam
I tend to go the air fryer route.

Pete
Nah. I'm a cooker and pan guy.

Bathtime

Sam
Let's take it to the bathroom.

Pete
If we must, but you stay on the other side of the door.

Sam
Do you like to run yourself a nice bath of an evening?

Pete

I must admit, I do love a bath. I love a good long, relaxing soak.

Sam

Do you light candles?

Pete

No candles, unless I'm planning on having a romantic wank. But when I have a bath, I like to open a bottle of red put on some nice emotional music in the background that promotes crying and lie there for an hour.

Sam

You don't just have baths in the evening, do you, Pete?

Pete

If I've got time, I'll choose a bath over a shower in the morning. But after a bath, I always get in the shower, 'cos you don't want to be lying around in your own shit, do you?

Sam

And what's your drying routine? Towel or hairdryer?

Pete

I just wander round the flat naked with my cock out. I air dry. I don't use a hairdryer or anything like that. It's a bit of a struggle, though. You can't sit down while you're air drying, especially with my dogs. So I'll often go out on the balcony after I've had a bath, and I'll air dry out there. Still naked. Having three fags.

Pre-bed routine

Sam
And what's your pre-bed ritual? Do you do certain things before you go to bed at night?

Pete
No. I just get in it.

Sam
You don't put any face packs on or anything?

Pete
No, I don't do any. Do you?

Sam
Yeah. Every night.

Pete
That's why Sam's got nice skin and I look like a fucking Chesterfield sofa.

Sam
I will cleanse my face in the shower. In a cold shower in the evening. I put cleanser on. Then I put on my hyaluronic acid. After that, I put on my Augustinus Bader Rich Cream. And then I put on a different moisturiser. Then I put on under-eye cream. A little bit of balm on the top.

Pete
Do you know what's mad? If people looked at us, they'd expect me to be the one that does all of that. They'd think I was the one who is all self-care and face masks, and you're the one just crawled out of bed. But nope, other way round.

My dream day? A Sam-free one!

Sam's Dream Day

Not that anyone is as interested in my day as they are in Pete's, but here goes: I'd wake up, then straight on the PlayStation, headset on. On the other end – Pete. We're playing *Call of Duty: Warzone* and he's taking it seriously: 'Right mate, we're going in hot. I've got your six.' That would make my day. Then we'd go to the pub, have a couple of beers... not sure what we'd do after that. But the most important thing would be waking up and gaming with Pete.

Of course, he's never touched a console in his life. Never. He thinks it's lame. He says it's childish. He needs to find his inner child. I think the TikToks are helping, actually.

22

Dating in the Public Eye

Dating is hard enough, but when you're in the public eye it's harder.

Pete
As I mentioned earlier, when I was on *TOWIE*, I was happy to share my dating life with the world 'cos I was in love, I was happy and I didn't really understand how interested people would be in our relationship. I was also so fucking naive about the way these shows worked and the way the press and public obsessed with our love lives. So, once I got my bearings and knew what I wanted out of this, I started to retreat a bit. These days, if I'm seeing someone, I make sure I do it in private so no one can comment.

Sam
I know what you mean. Even though creating content and being online is a big part of my daily routine and I love it, there are some things that you're not going to share.

Pete and Sam Write Each Other's Dating Profiles

Clearly, with all the relationship car crashes we've experienced over the years, we're not exactly experts in the dating field. But to help us find the one, we thought it might be a good idea to have a go at internet dating, and wrote a dating profile for each other.

Pete, 37 (with one foot in the grave)
PROFESSIONAL GRUMP | DOG DAD | GUINNESS GUZZLER

Right, I'm Pete. I say fuck and cunt a lot, I drink Guinness and would probably prefer to hang out with my dogs than you.

I hate most people, can't tolerate bullshit but love my mum and my best mate Sam, but that's about it.

I've got a body full of tatts, so if we ever get bored of chatting let me have a kip and you can spend a few hours trying to work out what the fuck some of them mean.

I give off this fuck-off attitude, but if I let you, you might discover that I actually have a heart of gold. Just don't tell anyone.

Can cook for one – a veggie stir fry is my go-to – but could probably stretch to two if you bring the extra noodles and lower your standards.

Hardly ever home as I've always got a bit of work on, so be prepared never to see me. So if you have a life of your own, that would preferable.

I'm a bit like a vampire – I don't sleep much, so the best time to catch me is 3 a.m. But I'm usually off out at 5 a.m.

Also, I'm almost forty and expecting the Grim Reaper to come knocking any day now. So if you're looking for a long-term relationship with a rosy future, you might want to look elsewhere.

Dealbreaker: If you date me, you date Sam. There will, I warn you, be three in this relationship. But no kinky shit. While we get it on, he'll be in a corner on his Gameboy.

Sam, 34 (mental age 12)
EMOTIONAL VELCRO | GAMER | CAT DAD

Hellooooo there, I'm Sam Thompson, former King of the Jungle, and I'm an irritating little prick!

When he's not walking his cat, dyeing his beard or spending a good forty-five minutes deciding which white T-shirt looks cool, Sam is actually a very sweet little beaver of a man. His heart? Definitely in the right place, even if his madcap mind is usually in Narnia or wherever the hell Dungeons & Dragons happens.

If you're an independent woman, Sam might not be the geezer for you, mainly because he loves to smother. Not in a serial killer way, but with love. We're talking full emotional Velcro. If you leave the room for five minutes, he'll probably send you a voice note asking if you still love him. But don't worry, you'll get some you time when he's distracted by something shiny, or is off playing Dungeons & Dragons – or whatever the fuck he plays – with his spotty teenage gamer mates from across the globe.

It might not look it, but Sam has a lot going for him. Thanks to a recent glow up, he's no longer a skinny streak of piss. However, he's as vain as fuck, so you'll have to beat him to the bathroom, where he spends most of his time slapping salmon spunk all over his puss. Oh, and if you're with him for years and he carks it, he's rich, so expect an impressive inheritance.

THE PRESS LOVE A COUPLE STORY

Pete

So what's changed between early Pete and present Pete? I still go out, still do what I want, still date – I just don't talk about it any more. It's all I ever used to get asked. Now, when I do interviews or anything like that, I just don't go there.

Other people in my position don't feel like that. Being in a couple can be financially beneficial, but that has never been the case for me. The press and the public love a couple story – and then a break up! But now I try to hold back. I don't have to share that part of my life for work. I want to be able to love and to hurt in private.

This fame game – it can consume you. And then you're left with nothing for yourself.

Sam

But you and I can still make cracking TikTok content. That's never going to change.

PETE AND SAM'S DREAM DATE

Sam

We get so many emails, letters and DMs from our *Staying Relevant* family, asking us what it would be like on our dream date. So we thought we'd answer some of your questions.

Pete

So where in the world would you take your perfect date?

Sam

An arcade. I love an arcade. A VR experience would be fucking great. An arcade experience, for me, is absolutely up there. Or a little cinema visit would never go amiss.

Pete
What are you, fourteen? Maybe you could just wander around the shopping centre.

Sam
Yeah, I would. I'm quite a basic dater, to be fair. As I said, an arcade would be lovely. A bit of Laser Quest, something like that. You know, I actually went climbing on a date not too long ago. It was a Clip 'n Climb.

Pete
Jesus. I'd opt for a cocktail bar with live music.

Sam
Jazz is lovely as well.

Pete
A nice bit of music in the background, somewhere you can actually sit and talk to someone. I don't want to do an activity. I don't care if you can climb. And going to the cinema – absolutely pointless. I'll tell you what, let's go out on a date to try and get to know each other, and sit in silence for two fucking hours.

Sam
But you do get that little hand-behind-the-back feel, you know, and you're like, Oh my God, I'm in.

Pete
One of the creepiest things you've ever said. I just want to sit and talk to someone, have a nice environment, dim lighting, something that feels romantic.

Sam
Tapas is great, because you tapas and then you tap ass.

Pete
Consensually, of course.

Sam
And what would you wear? Have you got a seduction outfit?

Pete
I just wear black generally, on dates. Go black. Nice, plain, simple. I make an effort, so I wear shoes. I don't wear trainers. Sam loves a trainer.

Sam
I do love a trainer. I wear a high-top sometimes.

Pete
And nothing will be ironed. Although he's recently got a stylist, spent a lot of money in Selfridges and on Mr Porter, and now he looks great. So at least the creased clothes will look good.

Sam
I might wear a shirt on a date, you know.

Pete
I'll probably always wear a shirt and smart shoes. Every five years, Sam buys a pair of shoes, a pair of boots. They're always from Russell & Bromley. He'll wear them until he's ripped the arsehole out of them and then he'll buy a new pair, and that's what he considers a smart shoe.

Sam
Nice sandy-coloured Chelsea boot, or black leather. It's my vibe. Seduced already. Sometimes a shirt, but recently the shirts are too small.

Pete
What he's done there is he's basically said they're too small because he's now jacked. They don't fit his fucking chest.

Sam
Me and Pete went out recently, and Pete looked at me and went, 'Oh dear, you're bursting out of that shirt.'

Pete
Sam has obviously been working out, because he's in his glow-up year at the minute. And actually, I'm going to be really honest: I'm finding it quite annoying. I used to be the attractive one because he looked like shit. Now I'm his ugly drunk little mate. And this geezer, with all his hydrochloric acid, his stylist, the old mullet – he's the heartthrob and people look at me like I'm chopped liver.

Sam
Oh Pete! The girls all love you.

Pete
Going back to the date, how would you end the night? With a kiss or a hug and a handshake?

Sam
Love a kiss, love a snog. I might go, 'I'm having a really good time.' And they'll hopefully say, 'I'm having a good time,' so I'll I go, 'Look, I'm gonna be honest with you. I've been thinking this for a while – I'd love to kiss you.' That way, you get the go-ahead. The last thing you want is a rejection. Because I never know whether to lean in or not. And people talk about the 70/30 rule.

Pete
What the fuck is that?

Sam

When the kisser leans in 70 per cent and the other person has the choice to lean in on the last 30 per cent or not at all. It can be great, and it can be awful at the same time. So I'm straight up. Just ask.

Pete

It all depends on the date and how it's gone, because you can't pre-plan that. Though I've never had a bad date, mainly because you can learn something from anyone you meet, whether you get on with them or not. But generally it will end up in a kiss. Or something.

Sam

And what about after the date? Do you text straight away or leave them hanging? I'd text them the same night. I want to show I'm keen.

Pete

Sam has got no kind of gameplay whatsoever. Actually, it's not even gameplay – there's no game whatsoever.

Sam

I'm straight in that night, asking, 'How did you find it? I had a great time. When are we seeing each other again?'

Pete

Then he'll send them a questionnaire about how the date went. Whereas I'll message them when I next think of them. Whenever that is – maybe never.

FAME'S BROUGHT A LOAD OF SHIT THAT'S MADE DATING HARD

Pete

Now I'm older, it does get harder to meet someone because there's all that shit already out there about me. It's difficult to find someone who doesn't come in with a preconceived idea of who I am. I don't think my past has helped me, for a number of reasons.

Fame's brought a load of shit that's made dating hard. Most people have a 9 to 5, they've got weekends free, a bit of routine. I could be away for a month or two, or heading to a live Saturday-night television show on a random weekend. It's all a bit unpredictable. So, if someone's not part of that world, it's hard to make proper time for each other. But then, if they are part of that world, it's nearly impossible to keep anything private or make diaries work. So basically, I'll die alone. Well ... actually, me and Sam will probably just die together, I imagine.

Sam

I'll be right by your side, mate. Literally by your side.

Pete

Not necessary! The funny thing is, this fame lark makes it a bit easier for me to meet people, as it's a sociable job. But keeping people? Actually making things work? That's a different story.

It makes you wary of making mistakes. And even if you don't make one, the headline becomes the truth, no matter what happened.

Sam

You mean all those times we've been linked to women who we were just talking to?

Pete
I had something happen to me a few years back which still boils my piss. I was doing a PA at a club up north somewhere and got chatting to this girl, who told me that her sister had died and that every year she and her mates marked the anniversary by throwing an event or something. Then she starts showing me pictures of me with her sister at a PA, telling me I'd met her a few times. 'She loved you,' she says. Because I couldn't hear her properly in the club, I asked her to step outside with me for a fag.

Outside, she tells me she's set up a foundation in her sister's memory. I was pretty moved by the story, and as she seemed genuine I sent her over some money to help with the foundation. She starts bawling her eyes out because she's so grateful. It was a really sweet, emotional moment, and I was so glad to be able to help. Anyway, next day? Headline: Pete Wicks in blazing row with mystery woman seen crying in smoking area. Pictures of us hugging, looking serious, whatever. Just complete bollocks.

NOW SAM'S SINGLE, HE'S GETTING ATTENTION IN A WAY HE'S NEVER HAD BEFORE

Sam
After I split from my ex at the start of 2025, I have attempted to date other people, but it's been harder than I thought. Back in *MiC* days, who I was dating flew pretty much under the radar. But since *I'm a Celeb*, things have changed considerably.

Pete
His stock has risen in the fame game. And now he's single, he's getting attention in a way he's never had before. Just for going on dates. Just for liking a picture. He was in the

paper the other week with someone, but he hadn't even done anything, he just liked a picture on her Insta. I've had that daily, but for Sam, it's all new.

Sam

I went on a date with one girl and was racking my brain to think where we could go that was quiet. I ended up saying to the girl, 'You're going to have to go in before me, and we can't leave together.' But then Pete said not to overthink it that much. Just crack on. Don't say anything. Don't explain. Just go.

Pete

You see, Sam is all cloak and dagger, turning up to dates in bloody disguises. It's not that he isn't a ladies' man, in spite of his dodgy barnet, his irritating personality and his bad breath . . .

Sam

Oi, I don't have bad breath.

Pete

I know you don't, but I thought I'd chuck in something different. In spite of all that, he does all right with the ladies. It's just that the press didn't used to care all that much. No one gave a shit who Louise's little brother was dating until he became Sam Thompson, King of the Jungle.

Pete's Dating Helpline

Even though Sam has been in relationships, he doesn't know how to date as I have him on the phone all the time, asking me for advice about what to wear, where to go, all that. Here are some of the messages.

> I'm a bit nervous today

> Don't overthink it, mate. Just enjoy it. The press will do what they want anyway, so you can't live by them. Just go and have a good time

> Thanks, mate. Do I wait for her inside? Less chance of anyone seeing. Or is that overthinking it?

> Yes, that's overthinking it. Go inside, get yourself a drink and chill. Standing outside like a weirdo on the street is not the way to do it. Text her, ask what she likes to drink, and have it waiting on the table when she arrives

> Such a good idea. You give good advice

> When she arrives, say hello, all that jazz. Cheers to the good times, good days. Look her in the eye when you cheers her. Don't be a creep, don't stare. Tell her she looks stunning. You know this stuff

No, I don't. So what do I say? Do I mention her hair or eyes?

> Whatever you genuinely think, mate. Just enjoy it

You know I'm going to say something creepy. I just know I am

> Also - don't go in for a hug. Kiss on the cheek. It's more intimate. A hug's what you do with your nan

So don't hug, kiss her. Just go for the cheek?

> Yeah, cheek's fine

We're dating, baby

> Forget the press and being seen – just enjoy it. You might actually like her. Don't talk about yourself too much. And stop saying you don't know what you're doing – be a man

Told the restaurant I'm on a date. They gave me a window seat. Terrifies me. Can I move?

> I'm not there, mate. If you want to move, ask them. Why did you say you're on a date anyway? You're fine. No one cares what you're doing

I panicked. Didn't want to sit at a shit table. So now I'm in full view of everyone
Beer's never gone down so quick. I'm early

> How early are you?

45 minutes. Done all the drinks now

> If you're 45 minutes early, why would you order the drinks?

Because you told me to

> Yeah, but I meant when she's about to arrive – not now

> You said it

> Yeah, but I thought you meant she was going to be there soon

That's what I have to deal with on a daily basis.

Sam's Dating
Advice for Pete

Pete, you're a great guy, but I think you make it hard for yourself. What you need is someone with her own stuff going on. You're perpetually busy, but I think you keep yourself that way on purpose. So you don't have to commit. You need someone as busy as you are. Someone who literally doesn't have time for you – in the best way.

You have to face up to the fact that you are scared of commitment. When you've been single as long as you have, it must get hard. I think it was Tom Hardy who said, 'Be afraid of being on your own for too long – you'll realise how amazing your own company is.' And it's so true. Once you get comfortable being alone, it's hard to let in someone who might shake that up. So, take your time to look for someone who isn't needy, is independent and has a life of their own, a woman who understands that you are your own very unique and solitary man.

What are you talking about? Maybe...

Wise geezer

Pete's Dating Advice for Sam

Okay, Sam, first things first: you've got to stop panicking every time you send a message to a girl, all right? They can smell desperation a mile off. Stay calm. Be confident. Try to look and sound like you know what you're doing. Now you've had those teeth done and you've bulked up, you're looking good, you're funny - kind of - so own it.

When you meet for the first time, just relax. Try not to be too you. *— what do you mean?* By that, I mean don't be TikTok Sam. Don't smother her and jump all over her like a lovesick puppy. Breathe deep and breathe slow. I would say try to be aloof and create a bit of mystery, but I know what you're like - within five fucking minutes you'll be telling her your innermost secrets. Whatever you do, don't bombard her with geeky facts about your gaming mates in China. Leave that for a later date, or better still, never. Don't be afraid to let a bit of silence hang in the air, either. It makes you sound more confident and will give her poor lugholes a rest.

Last thing, mate: if she doesn't text back straight away, don't spiral. Play it cool.

Send one message - just the one - and wait. Don't start bombarding her with messages.

Bottom line: you've got this, Sam. Just be less... well, you, but in the best way.

All right?

23

Getting the Look

Surviving the spotlight and looking good doing it.

MORE THAN JUST TALENT

Sam
When you find yourself in the public eye, you've got to start thinking about more than just the work you do.

Pete
Or the lack thereof.

Sam
It's about how you present yourself. It's part of the job.

ALWAYS IN PETE'S STYLE SHADOW

Sam
Pete's always been a smart bastard. Great style, effortless cool. I spent years in his style shadow.

Pete
Some of us have it naturally. Others have to work a bit harder.

Sam
Thanks for that.

Pete
But fair's fair, you're looking great these days. Though there was only one way you could go, to be honest.

Sam
Er... thanks, I think.

Pete
Let's be real. The transformation's been something else: from a skinny snaggletooth in Chelsea to a gawky loser with ceramic teeth in your late twenties, and now you're rocking a dyed beard and a thinning barnet.

Sam
Dare I say, I'm looking good.

Pete
I'm not arguing. You're coming into your own, mate. Full glow-up. And I'm here for it.

POST BREAK-UP BOUNCE BACK

Sam
I'm definitely making more of an effort these days.

Pete
He clocked after his break-up that he looked pretty shit and needed to get back out there. So he's at the gym, trying to dress better, got himself a stylist who tells him what to wear.

Sam
And I'm looking good for it.

Pete
Even if most of the time it's just a white T-shirt.

Sam
Yeah, but a really nice white T-shirt.

Pete
And you need a stylist for that?

Sam
Just to get inspired.

STEALING FROM THE BEST

Pete
So who inspired the earring and the mullet, then?

Sam
You know who...

Pete
Roman Kemp, your nemesis!

Sam
When I saw him at the BRITs, I said to him, 'I want your head. I want your mullet. I want your earring.' And voilà – I did it.

Pete
All you need now is his career.

Sam

I'm working on that.

MULLET VS HAIRLINE

Pete

Look, I'm here for the mullet, honestly. But being real – not sure it's the best idea. You haven't exactly got a lot of hair to spread around.

Sam

True, that could be an issue. But there are ways around it.

Pete

Oh yeah? When are you booking yourself in for that procedure?

Sam

Nothing planned yet. But keep an eye out for the moment I start wearing caps.

WE'RE SO VAIN

Sam

Doing what we do for a job, we have to be a bit vain. Gym memberships, skincare, good clothes. We've got to keep ourselves looking pristine, because there's always someone younger, better-looking and funnier coming up behind us.

Pete

Don't I know it! I started at the gym a while back myself. Didn't want to look like a lump of dough rolled out.

Sam

Still can't get my head around you putting on a gun show!

Dare I ask if your recent gym visits are anything to do with you being a little bit insecure about your body compared to mine?

Pete
Well, I wouldn't exactly say that. I just wanted to get myself sorted out.

Sam
Hang on, didn't you say a while back, 'I can't let this happen! I can't have Sam looking like he does.'

Pete
I don't think I did.

Sam
Oh yes you did! I'll get Producer Pippa to play it back to you.

Pete
Well, let's just say you might have inspired me. A little bit.

Sam
Oh really? So do you do what I do in the gym?

Pete
Like what?

Sam
Like start off with ten reps on the dumbbell bench press?

Pete
You what?

Sam
Followed by ten reps on the preacher curl.

Pete
Erm . . .

Sam
Ten box jumps? Ten pull-ups?

Pete
No one likes a show-off.

Sam
So what *do* you do? Give us your gym timetable.

Pete
I'll get up after a night of sleeping badly. Then I have a coffee, three fags. Stick my porridge on.

Sam
And then you go to the gym. What are we doing?

Pete
I get to the gym very, very early. Around 5 a.m. I do about forty-five minutes on the rowing machine. But I split that in two: do twenty minutes, go outside, have three cigarettes, come back in, and finish the last twenty-five minutes. I'm not exactly a fitness influencer, am I?

Sam
It's actually pretty good for you.

Pete
I'm just trying to hold off death a bit longer. Give myself an extra two years.
I'll do a bit of free weights but not too much, and do 5k on the treadmill. I'm just trying to get rid of the Derby Kelly [Belly]. I still have a bit of an issue though, especially with

weights after I hurt myself on *SAS*. My left rib's still not right, so I can't do anything above my head.

Sam
I'd love to be your gym buddy.

Pete
I've told you before – NO WAY!

Sam
But I'd be a great spotter, and I'd be good at encouraging you. I'd walk around, help you with the weights, and be like, 'Three more reps, Pete. You've got this!'

Pete
Never!

Sam
One day I will just rock up to your gym and surprise you.

Pete
And I'll make sure security chuck you out.

Sam
Another important question – gym gear?

Pete
Usually a cut-off Harley-Davidson T-shirt, to make sure the guns are out. Black shorts. Nothing fancy.

Sam
You say that, but I bet everyone reading this book will find it all so interesting. What's on the old playlist?

Pete
My motorbike playlist. Whitesnake, 'Here I Go Again'. And while I listen to that, I do a bit of triceps, bit of bicep curls. I'm fitter than I look. Weirdly enough.

Sam
You always have been. Fit for a man who smokes and drinks like you.

Pete
Yeah. I should be dead.

PROCEDURES

Pete
I think we can all agree that Sam is looking mighty fine.

Sam
Why thank you, Pete, I appreciate your kind words. But where is this going?

Pete
Well, you've recently transformed yourself the natural way – gym, healthy diet and all that malarkey – but there was a time when you underwent some procedures to enhance your look.

Sam
I did and I'm not ashamed of it. Though I would be reluctant to have them now.

Pete
Take us through some of stuff you've had done.

Sam

Well, my teeth, obviously, which I got done when I was twenty-three and first made some money. I have no regrets about that in the slightest, because they look awesome. I had Botox once. Well, twice actually. Once during *Made in Chelsea*. My girlfriend at the time asked me to go with her and I was like, 'Why not?' Worst idea ever! I did a scene straight after and couldn't move my face. Everyone was like, 'What's wrong with you? You literally can't move your face – you look really weird.'

I swore I'd never do it again. But then I did have it again – I thought maybe I should, for preventative reasons. Again, bad idea. My face is too expressive. It looked like it was melting. So I won't be doing it again. But I *have* had salmon sperm under my eyes – that actually helped!

Pete

And what about the barnet? When you went that shit brown colour before the Soccer Aid match. It's settled in now, but Jesus Christ it looked a state.

Sam

It was very dark brunette. Almost black.

Pete

I didn't know you'd had it done until I got a load of messages and pictures sent to me about your appearance on *This Morning*. I mean, what were you thinking?

Sam

I got my hair dyed just after I did the UNICEF challenge and didn't realise I had *This Morning* two days later. Turns out it takes a couple of days for the colour to settle in. And it looked ...

Pete
It looked like you'd stuck your head in a bucket of shit.

Sam
It wasn't that bad.

Pete
Sam, it was! But it looks better now.

Sam
I got hammered by the public for it too. The comments I got were wild. No one mentioned the charity – just called me a vampire. Even lovely Ben Shephard looked at me and went, 'Oh . . .'

Pete
Which is not the reaction you want.

Sam
But I'm not the only one who's had a hair transformation. You've had your Pirate Pete locks chopped off after many years. Is there anything else you'd have done?

Pete
Well, aside from replacing vital organs that I may have damaged by years of partying, I wouldn't do too much. Although, Liv Attwood told me I should have my eyes done.

Sam
Your eyes?

Pete
Yeah, she says they're a bit saggy, which I have noticed now she's said it, and it comes as no surprise as I've nearly got

one foot in the grave. So maybe I'll have that done. Liv says she can introduce me to the right people. If anyone knows a good surgeon, she would.

24

The Benefits of Fame

Fame isn't just about money and attention. Sometimes it opens doors to incredible experiences, events, opportunities we'd never have dreamed of.

Pete
So what are the benefits of being famous? Money? The adulation? Nah, I'm not gonna lie. For me, it's the experiences that come with it. The things you'd never do in normal life. Like getting dropped on a desert island for a TV show or being put through your paces by a bunch of SAS lunatics. That's the proper good stuff. It's not the red carpets or the free cocktails.

Sam
Come off it, Pete. You love a bit of attention.

Pete
I gotta admit, I have had some mad perks, like getting let off a parking ticket, and someone buying me a drink just 'cos they recognised me. And of course being famous gives me a platform to talk about serious stuff.

The lifestyle's great, sure, but I reckon I'd have had a decent life if I'd stuck to what I was doing before. All the flashy, materialistic crap? That's just bollocks, really. It doesn't sit well with me. Why do I deserve to have that, just because I'm on the telly? If it's a job, that's okay. But if it's just, 'You can have this because you're famous,' sod that! No thanks. I find it odd. Some people, even people who do up their houses and whatnot, everything's gifted. 'Thanks so much to Dunelm for me vase …' You're living in a £2 million house – buy your own vase. I think some people treat it like a game, like, 'Let's see what I can get away with.' 'Massive thanks to Next for my flannels' – buy the fucking flannels.

I hired a couple of designers to sort my flat out ages ago and I was the one paying for all the stuff they picked out. I'm not about to sit there saying, 'Cheers for the new lamp, I love it.' If I loved the lamp badly enough, I'd have bought it myself. Know what I mean?

Don't get me wrong, the odd discount is nice. But even the little stuff, like someone saying, 'Don't worry about the car wash, mate' – nah. I want to pay for it. I respect what you're doing, 'cos at the end of the day, that's your job. And I want to treat it like a job. I don't want special treatment, I just want to pay for the service.

Sam
Speak for yourself. I love a freebie.

Pete
Yeah, you love it. You live for it. That's why you're so bloody rich. Me? I'd rather just pay my way and be done with it. Seriously, I get offered free holidays to the Maldives about fifteen times a year. I've been sent a year's worth of cleaning products. I am happy to pay for it myself. I don't want someone giving me stuff just because I'm on the telly.

And if that wasn't bad enough, I sometimes get sent stuff because some PR mixed me up with Joe Wicks. Joe fucking

If you don't want it, feel free to send it my way!

Wicks! I mean, come on – I look like his afterbirth. It's like a before-and-after photo, but I'm what Joe would look like after years on meth.

Sam
Well, now you're going to the gym and you've had your hair cut, I can kind of see it.

Pete
Only if you squint. Not that it stopped this one geezer coming up to me in the street thinking I was him. 'Oh my God, it's Joe Wicks!' he says. And I'm standing there thinking, *Really*? I went, 'Nah, not me.' He goes, 'Oh, come on, I know you're trying to keep it quiet.' I'm like, 'No, genuinely, it's not me.'

'Yeah, yeah, stop being humble!' Mate, it's not humility, it's just not me. So I tell him, 'I'm Pete Wicks.' And he says, 'Who?' Er, cheers, mate. I should've just gone along with it, to be honest. Saved myself the grief.

SAM'S PROBABLY SOFTENED ME, MADE ME A BETTER PERSON

Pete
If there is one benefit of fame – and this is where I might end up sounding a bit fucking soppy – it's that every so often you do come across some top people. I've met Vicky Pattison, Liv Attwood, Joe Marler. And, of course, my foray into showbiz is the reason I've got Sam in my world. And while I spend my waking hours slagging him off, I can't deny that he is my best mate and the best thing that's come my way since I entered this mad world.

It's been about six years since we met and I've definitely seen a change in the person I am. Yeah, I'm still a bit of a cunt, but now I'm a softer one. And that's down to Sam.

We balance each other out. That's a big part of why we're friends. People reckon we're not really mates, that we're just a funny TV double act, all surface, all for show. But nah. That fucking prick calls me three times a day, to tell me he's got a headache or ask which T-shirt he should wear. And I'm like, 'I don't care. You're a grown man.' But that's not for the cameras – that's real friendship.

As I say, Sam's helped me let go of the reins a bit. And I've given him some structure, support and guidance he probably never had before.

So, if you're asking why we're even friends – and I can't believe I'm about to say this. What the fuck has happened to me? – I'm the yin to his yang.

Sam
Yes you are, baby!

Pete
And that is why we have lasted so long in this industry. We're a team, a partnership who support each other and each of us brings something different to the party. When I don't know what I'm doing, Sam will be there to push me and come up with ideas that keep us moving forward.

Sam
I love pushing Pete. He doesn't know how good he is. But I do. I think if I wasn't here, he'd still be where he is today. Just not wearing inflatables in TikTok clips. He has ambition, even if says he doesn't. He's achieved so much – like being the proper business brains behind the production company. He might say he doesn't know what he's good at or that he's still to achieve something, but he's found his place. I think maybe I've just helped him find his path a bit quicker.

Pete
I agree. At the start of all this, I didn't know where this showbiz journey would take me. But thanks to Sam, he's dragged me along, given me a taste of what can be achieved, and now I feel happier about who I am. You see, teamwork is probably the most essential factor to achieve success. My strengths are where he falls short. And my weaknesses? That's where he's strongest.

IT'S IMPORTANT FOR ME TO FEEL LIKE THERE'S PURPOSE IN WHAT I DO

Pete
I know how lucky I am. I could be doing a real job. A proper hard job. Or struggling. So this isn't some 'woe is me' pity party – far from it. But that's sometimes tricky to get across on paper. People might read this and think I'm ungrateful, but I'm not. Don't get me wrong, I'll happily take the money that comes with the career I've somehow blagged. But do I deserve it? Absolutely fucking not. Don't be stupid. Why would I?

Sam
Well, Pete, this is where I beg to differ.

Pete
What do you mean?

Sam
Well, once upon a time I think you could say that you were making good money for just showing up and being you.

Pete
Yeah, being paid to be me. Pathetic!

Sam

But look how things have changed. Look how far you – we – have come. How much we have achieved. Long gone are the days when we'd have sold our arses to try to land another telly gig or to make a few bob. Over the years, you have worked super hard developing yourself as a legit podcaster and producer. You've written a bestselling book, produced and presented your own telly shows, you've launched your own company, we've won awards. We've achieved so much. Not bad for two reality tossers who basically spent their early years blagging their way around the industry.

Pete

Fair dos. I will admit, I am proud of everything I do. And it's probably only now that I appreciate what we have achieved. After years of thinking what I did had no merit, I realise that I've finally found what I really want to do. I love all these creative avenues that working with you has opened up. And I will admit, there was a time when I was embarrassed about being famous for just being me, because I didn't think I deserved it. That's why I did so much other stuff outside of it. Like the charity work, supporting good causes like the Humane Society International, the Dogs Trust, the RSPCA, Coppafeel, to name a few. It's always been important for me to feel like there's purpose in what I do.

Sam

Fuck me, this is getting a lot more serious than I thought it was gonna be.

Pete

Well, I wanted this book to have a little bit more to it than most podcast books. I wanted people to see that we have worked hard to get where we are. We didn't just show up and become an instant hit. We had to knuckle down and work hard, do some shit jobs, but always with the view that one day we would end up doing something we actually liked doing. And we have. I will admit, I am enjoying what we do, but I still can't get my head round the fame aspect of it. That's the bit I still find hard to deal with.

Sam

Whereas I'm pretty much the opposite. Being famous – or at least living this weird showbiz life – is what I love to do. I genuinely can't imagine doing anything else.

Pete

I mean, can you picture Sam working in an office, nine to five?

Sam

I'd be great! I could do the office.

Pete

Sure, whenever you made it in. And when you did rock up you'd be fucking around, eating people's food and moaning about your hair. You'd have to strap him to the fucking desk. There's no way he could sit still for that long.

It'd be hellish for everyone else too. People always say to me, 'Oh, I'd love to be around Sam, he's so fun.'

No, you wouldn't. Not all the time. 24/7? No fucking chance. The geezer is a helmet. You wouldn't want to be around him constantly. It takes a special kind of patience, and that's why this career of his is the best thing he could possibly be doing ... and probably the worst thing I could be doing. You know what I mean? But fuck it. We're both doing it.

Part 5

Staying Relevant

25

Going Legit

After almost ten years of brand-building and getting our names out there, we finally became credible when the dancefloor and the jungle came calling, changing our lives for ever.

Pete
After around ten years of doing practically every reality show under the sun, Sam and I got asked to do the two shows that most people would give their left nut for: *I'm a Celebrity … Get Me Out of Here!* and *Strictly Come Dancing*.

Sam
Both shows have been on telly for ever and still pull in massive viewing figures – even in these bleak old days for TV. They're the shows every ambitious – or thrill-seeking – celebrity wants to get on.

Pete
Partly for the experience, but mostly for the doors they might open. Sounds cynical, I know, but that's just the way it is.

Sam

If you go into the jungle and do well, you suddenly become part of the ITV family. Next thing you know, you're on *This Morning* (see: Vicky Pattison, our Sam), or *Loose Women* (Frankie Bridge, Olivia Attwood), and then the next thing you know, you're fronting your own shows like Joel Dommett.

Pete

Strictly does the same thing, but in a different lane. It introduces you to a new demographic: a bit older, a bit more discerning. Any work that comes off the back of it might feel a little more ... cerebral. Guest-hosting *The One Show*, maybe. Or popping up on that weekday morning show that isn't hosted by Ben Shephard and Cat Deeley. Which makes a change from getting your knackers out on a naked dating show in the Caribbean.

Sam

As I've said, the jungle was my dream ever since I was a kid.

Pete

Whereas I'd never considered making a tit of myself on telly in a sequined blouse. But look what happened.

PAY ME A QUID, I DON'T CARE. IN FACT, I'LL PAY YOU. JUST LET ME DO IT

Sam

It's been almost two years since I was crowned King of the Jungle, and I still can't believe it. Actually, forget about winning: I still can't believe I was there in the first place. Being in the jungle was never part of my career plan. It was the *dream* – which is a totally different thing. It was never in the plan because I never thought I'd be offered it. But it was always my dream.

I've watched the show since I was a kid, sitting in my parents' living room. I was the biggest fan. I loved the idea of being dropped into the middle of this mad jungle with a bunch of celebs, doing those challenges. I couldn't get enough of it. The team who make the show are just so good at what they do. The production, the way it all works – it's incredible. I remember going out to Australia years ago to do *Extra Camp* and seeing how it ran, and I thought, This is phenomenal. I remember saying to myself then, 'If I ever get offered this show ... I'd just die.' But deep down, I never thought I ever would.

And then I got the phone call from Seb and Jonny, my managers at Insanity.

Now, you hear all this stuff, right? 'So-and-so got a million quid,' blah blah blah. When they called me, I was like, 'Pay me a quid, I don't care. In fact, I'll pay you. Just let me do it.' I just wanted to be part of it. I was over the moon.

Pete
When Sam got the job, he cried like a fucking baby. Then he started to overthink how he should be when he got in there. He kept asking me whether he should calm down who he is, whether people would like him. Even though I knew he was going to be more irritating than a dung beetle in your undies, all I ever told him was, 'Just be yourself. If people don't like it, they don't. If they do, they do. But if you're the person I know you to be, you'll win it.'

Sam
Which was the loveliest thing to hear!

Pete
And you know what? I knew he'd win. I just knew he'd end up being King of the Jungle. I even went on *Lorraine* and

called it. The lovely thing is, I don't think it even crossed Sam's mind that he could pull it off.

Sam

Genuinely, I thought I would be the last person to win it. There were so many other big characters in there, like Fred Sirieix from *First Dates*, Marvin Humes, Tony Bellew, Josie Gibson off of *This Morning*, Nick Pickard from *Hollyoaks*, Nigel Farage and Britney Spears's sister Jamie Lynn. You know – people who were proper famous.

I actually thought I was going to be one of the first out because I wasn't sure how the public would take me. I kept thinking back to my *MiC* days, when everyone was calling me a knob online. But as the days went by and campmates started to leave, I was just so shocked that I had lasted as long as I had. When we hit the final few days, I did start to wonder if I could make the final. But in my heart of hearts I was convinced that Tony would be the king.

I thought what I'd get out of the show was actually being there in the jungle, getting to do all the stuff I'd watched on the TV for years, and finally meeting Ant and Dec properly after chasing them up the red carpet at the NTAs!

Pete

But I had a feeling he was gonna do it – unless, of course, he said something stupid and got himself cancelled. Unsurprisingly, he was more annoying than I thought he'd be. And I think most of the campmates felt it. Especially poor Tony Bellew, who Sam latched onto like a fucking limpet, poor geezer. But if someone as pessimistic and miserable as me can learn to love someone who's as much of a cock as he is, then so can the rest of the camp and indeed the nation. Don't get me wrong – he's a bellend. But he's *my* bellend.

Sam
Mate, you say the sweetest things. You're like a modern-day Shakespeare.

Pete
Don't I know it. As they say, I know my fucking price, I am worth no worse a place.

Course I didn't just reel off this Shakespeare quote. Had to look it up, to sound like I know what I'm talking about

Sam
Eh?

Pete
You went to a posh school, you should know that!

Anyway, I think the jungle was really good for Sam, because it gave him that overall validation, something he probably never had before.

Sam and Pete's Jungle Diary

Landing in Australia and lockdown life

Sam

I thought spending two weeks in the jungle was going to be the hardest part. But it turned out it was tough from the moment I landed in Oz. When you get there, you go into proper isolation for a full week.

It's military-grade lockdown. You can't tell anyone you're even there. But you know me, the first thing I do is blow it. Put my size tens right in it. I landed at Brisbane airport and there were paps everywhere. I was like, Well, they know why I'm here.

Journalists were shouting at me, asking, 'Excited to be going into the jungle?' and I casually answered, 'Yeah, can't wait!'

'Looking forward to meeting your campmates?'

'Yeah, absolutely!'

I broke every rule and totally forgot what my publicist Charlotte had said before I left! As I got into the car, a journalist shouted, 'You know, you're the only one who's told us you're going in!'

As I got in the car, I sat back in the seat and went 'Fuck!'

Pete

You fucking prick! That's why you can't be trusted to keep anything to yourself.

Sam

Guilty.

Pete
And then they took your phone.

Sam
Yeah, so I had no phone, no internet, which was hard for me, as you can imagine. It's the biggest show you're ever going to do, and they just take your phone. You can't speak to anyone. You get homesick, and you're just stuck in a room for seven days. No internet. No phone. No loved ones. Nothing. And if you want to leave your room, you have a chaperone. Mine was called Trish. Lovely lady. Seventy-five years old but a proper spring chicken.

Seven days locked up with no contact with the outside world really gets to you, and you feel like you're already on another planet.

Entering the camp

Sam
My first day in camp, I felt like I was going to have a panic attack. I'd gone in buzzing, all guns blazing, but the minute I was there, it hit me like a truck. My heart was racing, I was sweating, and I really thought I was gonna throw up. The rest of the campmates kept asking, 'Why are you so quiet?' I was just overwhelmed.

Eventually, I settled in. Everyone was so nice, and you sort of forget you're even on TV.

Pete
You say everyone was nice, but not straight away. There were issues, weren't there? You were hugging people who didn't want to be hugged.

Sam
Was I? Name names.

Pete
Fred Sirieix, for one. Day one, you went in for a hug and he pushed you away.

Sam
I think he was too hot, 'cos he was decked out in a double-breasted jacket in the Aussie sun. Though he doesn't sweat, apparently. I thought we were going to be best mates, so I kept hugging him anyway.

Pete
You were hugging so many people that some clever bastard set up a Twitter account called Sam's Hugs, which was sending virtual hugs flying everywhere in your name.

Meeting Marvin – instant bromance

Pete
Everyone did fall in love with you, especially Marvin. He was like your little brother in camp. I wasn't sure what to make of it to start with, as he's such a geezer. I'd said to you before you left for Australia that I was worried was you'd find a bromance with him, and that he'd replace me. And then when Tony went in... well, I didn't know what to do.

Sam
When Pete and I finally reunited, one of the first things he said to me was, 'What's this about Marvin and Tony B?' I loved it, 'cos I knew we'd cracked him. Pete Wicks was jealous. I could see the pain in his eyes, the anguish in his face.

Pete
It wasn't that bad. I was actually kind of glad they'd taken you off my hands for a few weeks. I needed the rest.

Sam

Meeting Marv was massive for me. I've always loved JLS, I used to dance to their songs in clubs. 'Everybody in Love' is one of my favourite songs ever.

I think I made it really awkward for Marv to start with, so I started singing his own songs at him.

Pete

Which is the worst thing you can do to a pop star!

Sam

Marvin ended up teaching me the dances, probably out of pity. We had proper bromance vibes.

Pete

I actually learned that song and dance while you were in there too. I thought it would cheer you up when I came in to see you. They didn't show it on TV, but we did it in the jungle, and we were both crying.

Tony Bellew – the new Pete?

Pete

Then Tony Bellew came in – and it was game over for me.

Sam

Tony Bellew. T Bone. Teddy T. He was an absolute unit. Six foot four, manly 'tache, muscles on muscles. He looked like the kind of guy who chops down trees in his spare time.

Pete

So everything I'm not, then. I can barely prune a bush!

Sam

He was a proper geezer. The first task he did was drinking cow's anus smoothies.

Pete

Yeah, I could do that. I wouldn't, but I could if I wanted to.

Sam

But bless Big Tone, even he couldn't handle it and was gagging, throwing up all over the place. Nigel Farage, on the other hand, was knocking them back like lagers.

Pete

Well, he's a fucking rottweiler. Doesn't let anyone or anything faze him.

Sam

When Tony arrived in camp, I was buzzing. I ran straight up to him, stopped dead and said, 'Can I hug you?' He stood there like a statue: 'Yeah, all right.'

Pete

You looked like a kid at Christmas. Tony said afterwards that before he went in to the show, his chaperone had shown him the first couple of episodes, caught a load of you and said, 'Who the fuck is that?'

Sam

The first thing I thought was, You're my Pete Wicks. Old school. Hard exterior, soft interior. I stuck to him like glue and wore him down, and the real Tony came out. He's truly a lovely soul.

Pete

Poor fucker. I should really set up a support group for

victims of Sam Thompson's obsession. And then you slapped him.

Sam
Well, he had a mosquito on his forehead!

Pete
I thought he was gonna knock you out. I would've. But I have to admit, it was one of the best bits of TV, to see you slap him and then go, 'Well, that was quite dangerous, wasn't it?'

I REALLY DIDN'T WANT GO OUT THERE AS I'D MISS OUT ON LOADS OF WORK

Sam
Before I flew out to Australia, I knew Pete would be meeting me when I left the show.

Pete
And I was like, 'Oh, come on. Three weeks? It's a long time to be out there.'

Sam
And I said, 'Please. I need you to be there.'

Pete
Honestly, I felt forced into that bollocks. But what could I say? I really didn't want go out there as I'd miss out on loads of work. But my management encouraged me to look at it as a couple of weeks' holiday. It was nothing of the sort. I didn't realise I was going to be up on the Sunshine Bus at 4 a.m. every morning to go to the camp and sit with the friends and family. I don't even watch the bloody thing. So when it was on and they showed the friends and family, I'd

be outside having a fag. I couldn't bear it. Couldn't bear watching him aggravate the shit out of everyone.

What also pissed me off is that if and when your person gets kicked out, you get to enjoy the rest of your time in Australia at the luxurious Versace hotel. But I guessed the fucker was gonna win, so I'd have to wait three weeks. I had to stay there for the duration, losing a lot of work. But it was worth it.

Sam

Pete likes to pretend he doesn't care, but he does. When he came in to see me just before the end of the show, I swear I saw him cry.

Pete

Don't be a tit. I had a fly in my eye. It was you who cried. I remember, when he came around the corner and saw me, he just burst into tears. And it made me upset, because I'd never really seen that.

Sam

I missed home so much. Seeing you really hit me. When I saw you, I panicked.

Pete

You actually ran away at first, then came back.

Sam

When you said, 'We're proud of you,' I just lost it. I'd never had anyone say that before.

Pete

I was trying to tell you how well you were doing, that the public loved you. But it looked like I was attacking you, screaming, 'YOU'RE DOING GOOD!'

Sam

We just sat there, holding hands, crying.

Pete

It looked like a scene from *Brokeback Mountain*.

Sam

Honestly, it recharged me for the final days. I went back into camp so happy.

Pete

People see him as a bit of an emotional peach, but they don't see him sad or breaking down. I didn't expect it. I think it was just out of pure safety.

He'd spent weeks there. It's hard for someone like him, because he always feels like he has to entertain and blah blah blah. But he isn't like that all the time. He had down days. And he was stuck there, feeling like he had to constantly entertain everyone. I think when he saw me, he just felt, *Thank fuck.* He also had no idea how he was coming across on the telly. I think he just needed reassurance. And then, of course, the tosser went and won!

Sam

I couldn't believe I won the show. I felt so emotional. I mean, this was the show I had wanted to be on for years and then I went and won the damn thing. Words still fail me. But sitting on that throne was overwhelming. I just sat there thinking, Why me? What have I done to deserve this?

I'm actually very bad at receiving love or adulation. I felt so overwhelmed, because I couldn't believe people had voted for me. They had made the effort to sign up to the app, cast their votes. That meant so much.

But then I was excited to get out, 'cos I knew my best mate was there waiting for me. The first thing I did when

I saw Pete was jump on him. I basically dry-humped him on national TV.

Pete
And the bridge was wobbling, because you were jumping around like a fucking kangaroo. Before he crossed the bridge, the producers told everyone, 'Do not jump on the bridge.' First thing Sam does? Jumps. I had to hold on for dear life. Nearly fell off.

Sam
I was so pleased to see Pete again. I realised how important he was to me. But then I noticed that his face looked different. It looked like he'd had some work done while I'd been away.

Pete
Which I hadn't.

Sam
You looked like you'd had a load of fillers or Botox.

Pete
Well, if anyone can spot stuff like that, it's you, with everything you've had pumped into your face! It's true I did look a bit like Jackie Stallone, but I hadn't had a facelift. Got savaged by mosquitoes and was bitten all over my eyelids.

Sam
It was bad.

Pete
I looked like the Bride of fucking Chucky. Biggest moment of your career and there I am on TV, looking like I've been in the ring with Mike fucking Tyson.

Sam

Back at the hotel, everyone was celebrating, congratulating me and making a big fuss of me, but I just wanted to blend in, be part of the group. It's weird, sometimes I love being the centre of attention, but when it's put on me like that, I feel awkward. All I could think about was how much I had loved spending time with Tony and Marvin. One of the first things I thought was, I can't wait to do a TikTok with Tony.

Pete

Oh, so you weren't thinking of doing one with me, then?

Sam

Pete, you sound jealous. Are you jealous?

Pete

Course not. It would have been a fucking relief to have you off my back. Literally!

Sam

Mate, you know you're my number-one TikTok buddy. There's no one's back I'd rather ride on.

Pete

Thanks?

Sam

The other thing I was thinking was, I wonder if me and Dec are going to be friends now? And we are. Dec messages me sometimes, out of the blue, to ask how I'm doing, which is so lovely. And I always send back this massive essay, like, 'Hey man, I'm doing great, thanks so much...' Then I think, 'You've overshared so much.' I always ask him to play golf, which we haven't done yet.

When I was filming *Unpacked* last year, I went for

dinner with Dec and his wife. I totally crashed their date night. I was out there alone – everyone else had someone with them – and they were like, 'Do you want to come for dinner?'

I KNEW BEING ON *I'M A CELEB* WOULD CHANGE A LOT

Pete
I'd probably say I'm Sam's safety net for a lot of things. That's why he wanted me out there to greet him after he got out of the jungle. And it upset me, because I never really considered, with the ADHD, autism and everything else, that he always feels like he has to make people like him. I think that's why he broke down. Because he knows that, regardless, I love him. So he doesn't need to try.

Sam
Oh Pete, give us a hug!

Pete
Get off me. Well, he didn't need to worry, 'cos he fucking won. And he deserved it, because he's unusual, a breath of fresh air who was good to watch. Sam is, in my eyes, the perfect reality star turned broadcaster, to use a nice term. Because he's done it through hard work and personality. And you can't teach those things.

Sam
When I went in, I knew it would change a lot. Not just for me, but for Pete too. Whether he likes it or not, we're a duo. He doesn't always see it like that, which is weird, but I do. Pete and I are in this for the long haul. Whatever we're going to do, we're doing it together. I genuinely feel that way. And I don't think he realises just how much I love

working with him. When I was in the jungle, I remember thinking, This is going to be great for the podcast. It's great for us, for what we want to do together. Because that's the stuff I love doing.

And I'll never forget how, after I won, we sat outside the hotel having a cigarette and he turned to me and said something like, 'You're the nation's sweetheart now.'

He went, 'You don't understand how famous you are right now. But listen, I want you to go chase whatever dream comes from this. Don't worry about me. I'll be fine. Go do what you need to do.'

Pete
And I meant every word of it.

Sam
I know you did. But it made me so angry. I was like, 'What are you talking about? Nothing's changed. I don't understand why you're saying that.'

It was sweet, but I just didn't agree with it at all.

Pete
He said to me, 'I'm the same guy coming out of this as I was going in. In a year's time, someone else will win. Whatever comes from this, we're in it together.'

Sam
I would never want to do this alone. I hate the idea of going off and doing it all on my own. Pete was saying, 'Go on without me,' and I was like, 'No. I will drag you with me if I have to!'

Pete
After the show, he had so many opportunities coming in, and he kept telling me he wanted me to go on these fucking

things with him. But I was like, 'This is about *you*. I can't do everything with you. This is *you* that's done this. Don't worry about me. No one gives a fuck about me.' And I'm fine with that. We had got so used to doing things together up until that point, and I think it was really good for him to go and do something on his own, to smash the life out of it and kind of know his worth.

Sam
Pete, you're a superstar!

Pete
I think we had started to forget who we were. But him doing the radio and the jungle, and me doing *Strictly* and my radio show, and writing a book – doing things separately – really good for both of us. To remember we were individuals as well. I think you have to. Otherwise you become like the Chuckle Brothers, all that stuff.

I mean, you can still do that, but you need to have your own thing too. We work together, go out together. That's why we get on so well. He's so supportive of everything I do individually, as I am of him. And when you have your own thing, you can enjoy what you do together even more.

Sam
I do. I live for the stuff we do together. I wouldn't want it to end.

Pete
But the great thing that came out of his time on the show is that those people who thought we just do silly videos to make money could finally see we actually are best mates. That was a big moment for us, as people.

I DON'T THINK HE COULD TAKE IN THE FACT THE NATION HAD VOTED FOR WHO HE WAS

Sam

As euphoric as I was about winning *I'm a Celeb*, it hit me hard, I must admit. I hadn't expected to be King of the Jungle, and suddenly everything went into overdrive and I felt a bit lost at sea.

Pete

He was on such a high, I think he overworked himself. It was quite overwhelming for him. For him, it was a lot. It was demand, demand, demand. And it became about making the right choices, because suddenly he had so many more options.

Our friendship did change a bit in the weeks that followed. And what you tend to forget – especially with duos or couples in the same industry – is jealousy. One gets more popular and the other can't deal with it.

Sam

But that's not how it works with us. We're too different.

Pete

I used to get more attention than Sam, mainly from women. But post-jungle? Sam was like the fucking Beatles. We'd go out to places and we would have people come up and say, 'Pete, can you just take my picture with Sam?' I couldn't get a look-in. So I'd be there, taking pictures. I thought it was great. I was proud of him.

Sam

I'd won the biggest show on TV. I was doing so much stuff, so all of a sudden I was super busy!

Pete
He was everywhere, and I think it was a lot for him.

Sam
It was. I was going from here to there to everywhere, and I was doing it on my own. Pete wasn't with me, so I was constantly on the phone to him.

Pete
I tried my best to calm him down, saying, 'Mate, you'll be fine.' I don't think he really took in the fact that the nation – millions of people – had voted for him. For who *he* was.

Sam
He used to make jokes on the podcast, saying, 'It's hosted by Sam Thompson and the hairy mate no one knows.'

Pete
I loved that. He deserved it. And you know what? I think it probably brought us closer. It wasn't about me. It wasn't about us. It was about him.

Sam
But I still wanted to take Pete on the whole journey.

Pete
And I'd say, 'This is all you, man. This is all you.'

Sam
But I'd argue, 'No, this is us.'

Pete
And I'd tell him straight, 'They weren't voting for me. It's got nothing to do with me. This is you. You need to take this for you.' But he'd still say, 'No, this is us.'

Sam

Then, of course, it flipped after *Strictly*, and suddenly he was dragging me along. I remember saying to him, 'The only thing that's changed is more people will watch our videos now. More people will listen to the podcast. That's it. That's all that's different. We get to do more fun stuff together.' I said to him, 'If you think anything else is going to change, well, it's not happening.'

I know what I want to do, and I know who I want to do it with. And that's Pete.

26

Going Legit Part 2

IF YOU LIKE ONE OF US, GENERALLY YOU'LL LIKE THE DYNAMIC BETWEEN THE TWO OF US

Pete

Sam was right ... again. After the jungle, we had much more interest in the pod. The figures went up and more people came to our tours.

It was pretty obvious that lots of people had come to see the King of the Jungle – they'd all fallen in love with him. And then suddenly they were like, 'Oh, his mate's quite funny.' On the first tour, I used to open the show with 'Another fucking sold-out night. I presume 90 per cent of you are here for the King of the Jungle. I'm Pete. I've been his mate for a while. I'm pretty much the driving force behind everything he's ever done. But you won't know who I am because none of you give a fuck. So should we just give a round of applause for the King of the Jungle?' And they'd go mad for it.

Sam

Then we did another tour, after Pete's stint on *Strictly*, and it was the opposite. I would go, 'I am still King of the Jungle, but say hello to *Strictly Come Dancing*'s Peter Wicks...' and the crowd would go mad for that.

Pete

Weirdly enough, *Strictly* had the same kind of impact as Sam's jungle appearance, as it brought loads of new people to the pod. And those who hadn't already fallen in love with Sam, did. And vice versa. Because if you like one of us, generally you'll like the dynamic between the two of us. If you like me, then I'm still me with Sam. And if you like Sam, then you get the normal reactions of someone who thinks he's wild but loves him.

SAM SAW *STRICTLY* AS ONE THREE-MONTH-LONG TIKTOK

Pete

As I said, *Strictly Come Dancing* was never part of my career plan. Nor was it a dream.

However, my manager Gemma loved it and always wanted me to do it, so had banged on about it for years. I was like, 'I'm not doing it.' I just didn't want to, mainly 'cos I can't dance and didn't want to look like a tit. Then Gemma pitched me again, but didn't tell me, and the show's producers came back saying they were interested. Without even speaking to me, she said yes. When she told me, I tried putting up a fight but, in the end, I trust her judgement.

I had already filmed *For Dogs' Sake* – which was something really close to my heart – so my thinking was, if I do *Strictly*, it will help promote that show. That was the logic. But at the back off my head, I was also like, Well, I can't dance, I'll be fucking useless.

Anyway, a short while later we got a call asking me to come in for a dance test, where you spend an hour with one of the show's pro dancers to see how it feels. I did mine with Dianne Buswell, which is funny, because Chris McCausland – who ended up winning the show with Dianne – did his test with my eventual partner, Jowita

Przystał. I don't remember much about the test, other than being godawful. I was like a baby deer, my legs getting all tangled up. But – and I can't believe I'm saying this – when I came out of it, I called Gemma and said, 'Don't tell anyone, but I actually enjoyed it.' And that's because I like learning new things.

She went, 'Wait, so are you saying yes to me?' I was like, 'Look, I imagine they're not going to ask me. But yeah, if they do, fine, whatever.'

We didn't hear anything for a couple of weeks and eventually forgot all about it. Then one day Gemma called me and said, 'How's your day?' And I was like, 'Yeah, fine.' She said, 'A job's come in. It's going to take a lot of time and you'll be starting on 26th August ...' and she started rattling off details.

I cut in and said: 'Right, you keep saying all these things, but you haven't told me what the job is.'

'Oh yeah,' she said. 'You're doing *Strictly*.'

And that's when it hit me. I suddenly thought, Oh shit, I'm actually going to have to do it.

I called my mum and she pissed herself laughing. She went, 'No, you're not.' I said, 'No, I am.' She said, 'Fucking hell, that's going to be hilarious.' She also told me that she had sent me to a ballroom dancing class when I was about four. Which was news to me. She showed me a picture of me wearing a little suit. Apparently, I walked in and said, 'This isn't for me!' and then left halfway through the class.

When I told Sam he cried and said, 'This is gonna be so great for us.' And I went, 'Us? You're not fucking doing it.' And he was like, 'Yeah, but if you do well, I do well.' And I'm like, 'You fucking donut.' But he wasn't wrong, because he always thought I'd go far – at least to Blackpool, which I actually did. Surprisingly.

It's all he's ever wanted. As I said earlier, he has this weird fascination with watching me do things – mainly because

I'm useless. So this for him was like, 'This is just one three-month-long TikTok.' That's how he saw it. 'This is gonna be the best thing ever,' he said.

I ALWAYS TOOK *STRICTLY* SERIOUSLY. I JUST NEVER TOOK MYSELF SERIOUSLY

Pete
Right folks, for this section of the book I'm going to change things up a bit.

Sam
What do you mean?

Pete
Sam, you're fired!

Sam
What are you talking about? You can't carry on without me. We're team! I'm going nowhere.

Pete
Don't I fucking know it. No, I'm gonna bring in a special guest, just like we do on the pod.

Sam
Exciting! Who is it? Orlando Bloom? Daniel Radcliffe?

Pete
What do you think? I'm talking about someone who was on my *Strictly* journey...

Sam
Chris McCausland?

Pete
No, Jowita, you tit.

Sam
Yay! I fucking LOVE Jowita.

Jowita
Hey guys. Thank you for letting me be part of your book. I'm very excited to be in it.

Pete
So, in this chapter, we're looking back at my time on *Strictly*, and because I couldn't have done it without you, I thought it'd be a great idea to have you join us to talk about our time together.

Jowita
It's my pleasure.

Sam
Okay, let's take it back. When you first met Pete, what did you think?

Jowita
To be honest, I didn't really know who he was. As I'm Polish and I don't really watch telly, I didn't know what *The Only Way is Essex* was. But he seemed very nice and was very welcoming. It was also my thirtieth birthday, so it felt like a special day!

Pete
What a birthday gift I turned out to be – two left feet, and legs like a fucking chicken.

Jowita

I started teaching him a little bit of dancing. And I was like, Okay, he's actually not bad.

Pete

What you talking about? You could tell I was shit.

Jowita

Okay, okay, you were bad.

Sam

Brutal!

Pete

But true.

Jowita

There was nothing there. Absolutely no rhythm. Nothing. The one good thing you had was your feet. Your feet are amazing. You can go up on relevé and stay there – it's such a beautiful arch. I was in awe of your feet. I was like, 'Okay, we're going to use that. That's strength.'

Sam

I'm gonna look at your feet in a whole new way. Maybe you actually should stick them on OnlyFeet after all.

Jowita

Then I went home and did my research on Pete Wicks, and discovered what a character he is.

Sam

That's an understatement.

Jowita

But I'm not the type of person to believe everything I read, so don't I judge anyone until I get to know them. To start with I thought he was this very strong character, a confident alpha male who knew what he wanted. But once we started working together, I completely changed my mind and realised what a beautiful person he is, in terms of how much he loves learning new things.

Pete

It's true: when I put my mind to something, I give it my all. I felt more at ease because you were a great teacher. I knew my limitations, but I always took the show seriously, because if I'm going to do something, I give it 100 per cent.

Jowita

You were always there with me, totally focused. Never complaining. Never saying you were tired. I know that if we could rehearse more than eight hours, you definitely would have.

Pete

In a heartbeat!

Jowita

You were fully invested in it. I think that's because, first of all, you love learning new things.

Pete

I do.

Jowita

And second, I think you wanted to show everyone that you were capable.

Pete
I wanted to prove something to those people who reckoned I was gonna be out in week one or two, or thought I wasn't taking it seriously.

Jowita
I think your dedication and commitment helped us a lot, because there was definitely a struggle. Especially with rhythm. But you never give up.

Pete
I hate not getting something right. There were times when I used to think you were making the routines easier 'cos I couldn't do it, and I felt weird about it.

Jowita
The thing with you, Pete, is you are so talented and such an amazing person that I knew you'd be able to do everything I asked. It was just the time pressure. I needed to speed things up because we had to perform on the Saturday.

Sam
I remember when the first live show arrived, you were bricking it.

Pete
I was terrified. I really didn't wanna go the first week, and thought I wouldn't be good enough.

Jowita
What I discovered about Pete, that surprised me so much, was that he's not as confident as I thought he would be. He has a lot of insecurities – and I don't know why.

Pete

Well, I've said it time and time again: I don't think I'm enough.

Jowita

Before the first live show, I remember you were literally shaking, and I tried my best to calm you down. I said, 'You've done so much, you should be fine.' I knew you were so far out of your comfort zone and put it down to the fact that dancing is something you don't do every day. But then I realised it wasn't about the dancing. You just didn't want to let me down.

Pete

I didn't.

Sam

Aww, Pete I wanna give you a big Sam hug.

Pete

Get your hands off me!

Jowita

He didn't want to let me down. Not the audience, not the judges, just me. That was his fear. Which is kind of so beautiful. That made me feel like, Oh, okay. I see you.

Pete

I didn't miss a single day of rehearsals. Every week, I did the maximum number of hours they'd allow, no matter what else I had going on. In the first two weeks, me and Jowita were meeting at 5 a.m. We were getting dance halls to open early so I could train for eight hours before going off to do my show at the Hammersmith Apollo, which I'd been writing until 2 a.m. the night before. Then I'd be up again.

One of my best mates, Vicky Pattison, was getting married in Italy during the second week. I flew out to be there for less than twenty-four hours, and made up the time in other sessions. There wasn't a single week where I didn't max out my hours. And I was still working on everything else outside of *Strictly*. Still doing the podcast. Still filming other stuff. I was doing eighteen- or nineteen-hour days for three months. It was heavy. Really heavy.

I knew I wasn't the best dancer. I never claimed to be. But just because you're not the best at something, it doesn't mean you shouldn't try. I never stopped trying. I don't give up. Even when I'm godawful, I won't stop.

Jowita
Pete was fully committed. I never heard a 'no' from him. I never made it easy for him. I put him up in the air, hanging on a chain, going down into flames in a leather outfit... In Monday rehearsals, he'd come in and be like, 'Okay, what have you come up with this time?' Then I'd tell him the storyline, what we were going to do.

Pete
She'd say, 'You're swinging from the ceiling.' And I'd go, 'Don't be so fucking ridiculous.' Then I'd go outside, have a cigarette, come back in... and say, 'Come on then, let's do it.'

Jowita
Honestly, what we did, it's remarkable. I don't know if I'd have even been able to do it with a professional dancer. But I did it with Pete. The trust, that commitment and the connection we had, it was something else. That's what made us such a strong partnership.

Pete

During the series, we had some proper idiotic moments. The week I did *George of the Jungle*, I danced in a loincloth and started the routine balanced on Craig's desk, wiggling my bum around, before swinging myself on to the floor on a rope. Barefoot. When Jowita originally suggested all this to me, I just gave her a look and said, 'What the hell are you talking about?' But I did it anyway. For her. But secretly, I loved it. I even enjoyed wearing those pink latex trousers I had in Blackpool. I actually asked for them to be made tighter around the bum.

Jowita

One of the most stressful times for Pete was the preparation for the Halloween episode, where he was dressed as The Joker. In the week running up to the live show, nothing seemed to go right.

Pete

I couldn't get my head around the steps, no matter how I hard I tried. All week, the rehearsals were going shit. I genuinely thought I was going to be sent home that week, which made me even more upset. I kept thinking about my nan, who loved *Strictly*. That was an added pressure, because I wanted it to be perfect for her. I didn't want to let her down by being sent home. But Jowita encouraged me all the way.

Jowita

I believed in you. I knew you were going to make it happen. Because you always did. And you had so much support from people. But again, that fear of letting everyone down was getting in the way.

Pete

When it got round to the performance, my emotions took over and I remembered all my steps. It wasn't perfect, but when I'd finished, I was proud of myself and felt very emotional. I don't think anything danced more than my bottom lip.

Jowita

I think that moment brought us even closer. Like, no matter what was happening, you knew I was there for you.

Pete

I couldn't have asked for a better partner. I assumed the *Strictly* audience would look at me and think, Nah, not sure about him. Bit of a knobhead. The hair, the tattoos, the dry sense of humour – I thought they'd hate me. Properly hate me. But when I got saved by the public even though I knew I was rubbish, that was probably the only time I've ever felt overwhelmed by public support. It was my first time doing a show in which people had to vote. And I still can't believe that despite being one of the worst dancers from week three onwards, I made the semi-final. But that wasn't down to me, it was because people liked me and Jowita together. I owe a lot of that to you. Honestly. I reckon it was 90 per cent votes for you.

You dragged me through that show. Honestly, you're just unbelievable. To drag a fucking donkey like me through *Strictly* is mad.

Sam

You were great, mate. I said from the start that you'd get to the end.

Pete

Well, I didn't, did I?

Sam

No, but you went so far.

Pete

Each week, I'd feel guilty, because there were great dancers leaving. People who really cared. And here I was, still hanging on in there. But I did care. And I worked my arse off. It's just a shame that giving it 100 per cent doesn't make you better.

While I enjoyed taking part in the show, there were some hard moments. The press were brutal. I've never had it that bad. The *Strictly* curse bullshit too. At one point there were about thirty different articles in one week, asking if me and Jowita were an item. But the minute they started dragging my family into it, they crossed a line.

Jowita

Me, his team and his mum, Tracy, we all encouraged him to stick in there, telling him, 'Don't let them. Don't let them pull you down.'

Pete

I knew she was right. I couldn't let certain parts of the press or those fucking online trolls, who were sending me death threats, ruin it all. I couldn't let them take away this moment. Not just from me, but from Jowita, my mum, my agent, my team and my nan. And so I gave myself a good talking to and tried to ignore all the crap going on around me and focus on the job at hand.

However, there were still a few minor dramas that happened along the way. Luckily, it was the kind of stuff I can laugh about now.

Sam

Oh, are you going to tell everyone the story about me rocking up to your rehearsals?

Pete
No, this is my story! Why would I ruin it by putting you in it? So, during Movie Week, we were rehearsing the *George of the Jungle* routine when all of a sudden my front tooth popped out of my mouth. Just popped right out mid-dance. I picked it up, shoved it back in and hoped for the best.

Jowita
The next morning, he calls me really early and says, 'I swallowed my tooth. I was eating an apple, and I swallowed it.'

Pete
I panicked. How could I go on telly with a missing front tooth? I'd look like the old dad out of *Steptoe and Son*! Then I called my management team, anyone who'd listen, saying, 'Bit of a problem – I've just eaten my tooth.' Luckily my team are goddesses, and my PRs Charlotte and Megan remained calm, worked their magic and managed to hook me up with a dentist on Harley Street, who was able to rebuild my tooth and no one knew about the meltdown I'd had earlier in the week.

A dusty old sitcom from the seventies

Sam
Come on, Pete, tell everyone about my surprise visits.

Pete
Okay, okay, stay calm, you excitable little prick. As you can imagine, he just couldn't help himself, and made it his business to break in to my training.

Jowita
One time he turned up dressed as a tree. He was hiding in the bushes. I don't know what the purpose was, but he did that.

Sam

Just for the larks and for the 'gram!

Jowita

And then one day we heard that Sam and the *Staying Relevant* team were waiting in the car park to get into our rehearsal room. We were filming something for a VT and the production team were like, 'Wait, don't let them in until we're done.' Then, all of a sudden, Sam bursts in, dressed as a woman. With fake boobs, long blonde hair. I was like, 'What the hell is going on right now?'

Pete

I had to kick him out a couple of times because he was causing so much chaos. And then when he went back to his car, he set off the fucking alarm that disrupted everything at Elstree. The irritating little twat!

Sam

That day was hysterical. The look on Pete's face. I thought he was going to explode. Then kill me.

Pete

If there hadn't have been a camera there, I probably would have.

Sam

It was all jokes. I also remember the time Jowita kindly gave me a quick dance lesson and you looked like you were going to blow.

Pete

Yeah, 'cos, wouldn't you fucking know it, you picked up the moves really quickly, which did my head in.

Jowita

Yes, Sam, you were actually very good. You'd be great on *Strictly*.

Pete

Well, I've done it, so you can't now. So anyway, I banned him from rehearsals but he kept turning up anyway.

Sam

I always managed to find a way in.

Jowita

Pete was like, 'You're forbidden to come! We have to focus. I don't have time for this.' He was really taking the dancing part seriously and wanted to do well. Then whenever Sam turned up, everything shifted into fun mode and became a bit distracting.

Pete

I was trying to do a job and be professional, and this stupid tit is acting like a goat!

Sam

You loved it.

Pete

No, I didn't.

Sam

Yes, you bloody did.

Pete

No, *really*.

Jowita

Yeah, he would get annoyed, but deep down it was really nice for Pete to have him there. It was sweet.

Sam

Thanks, Jowita. See, Pete!

Jowita

Sam was there almost every week in the audience too. That was really special.

Pete

Yeah, I'll grudgingly admit it: it was nice to have you there.

Jowita

To get all sentimental, these guys are great together. They're very different, but I think what connects them is their big hearts. They're both very genuine, very loving and caring people, and very honest. It's just so beautiful that after all those years they're still such great friends. And I know they can count on each other. No matter what's going on, they'll always be there for each other. The support is out of this world. But I'm not surprised, because they're both very real, very genuine, and very caring. They do care about each other. A lot.

Sam

Jowita, that's beautiful.

Pete

Yeah, whatever. When we made it to the semis, I knew my time was almost up as the remaining contestants were just so good. As much as I was loving the experience, I was happy to leave, because I didn't think I deserved to go any further. But I'd promised myself from the start, I'd try to get Jowita to the final as she'd already choreographed the final show dance the week she met me, to the song 'Way Down We Go' by Kaleo.

Jowita

You see, when the celebs meet the pros at the start of the series, they give us a list of their favourite songs, something they'd like to jam to. And Pete's first song was 'Way Down We Go', which is one *my* favourite songs. When we started rehearsing, I said to Pete, 'Okay, we're going to do this in the final.' He just laughed and said, 'Don't be so ridiculous, we'll never make the final.' But I was adamant we'd get to there and said, 'Watch me.' I was always so sure we'd make it, but he was always like, 'No, we're going home.'

Pete

'Cos I was a fucking realist! And I was right. We never made it to the final.

Jowita

And so we didn't get to dance it, but I had choreographed it, had the costumes, concepts planned, everything.

Pete

I was gutted for her 'cos I knew how much that routine meant to her. And I promised her that one day we would perform the dance.

Jowita

Then one day Pete called me and said, 'I want to dance with you to that song. I want to do our show dance at the O2 show.' I was shocked at first, because I couldn't believe that Pete wanted to dance again! 'Are you okay?' I said. 'Did you hit your head?' He was like, 'What do you mean?' I said, 'You really want to dance again?' And he said, 'Yeah, I want to do it. If I'm going to dance with anyone, it's you.'

Pete
You deserved that. I wasn't good enough to give it to you the first time, so I gave it to you another way.

Jowita
When he called to ask me, I cried.

And then I said, 'All right, but what's the budget? I want flames.'

The show was spectacular. We outdid ourselves. I didn't even know if I could do it! But that's me and Pete. I think of something wild in my head, then try to make it happen on the floor.

Pete
And as those of you came to the O2 show know, the performance was brilliant. All thanks to my lovely friend Jowita, who is not only part of the *Staying Relevant* team, she's family.

MOST OF *STRICTLY* VIEWERS DIDN'T KNOW US AS 'THE CHEAT ON *TOWIE*' OR 'THE MORON FROM *MIC*'

Pete
I was over the moon I didn't make the final. Genuinely. I couldn't fucking dance. And let's be honest, the winner was obvious from the start. Chris was an amazing dancer. Fuck, he's an amazing man. Funny as fuck and a proper grafter. I love the geezer.

When I went out, I was happy with how far I'd got. I'd already got everything I wanted out of it by week one. Getting past the first week, that was my win. I wasn't first out. And then it just kept going. By the time we were halfway through, I was so far behind everyone.

But I was just ... me. Nothing special. Just shit. Not a trained dancer. Chris came on the podcast and I said to him, 'Mate, you fucked me here.' Because I thought the only chance I had of surviving week one was, I'll beat the blind guy. Turns out, none of us did.

Throughout the show we had such a laugh, pure banter. I used to say to him, 'You can see, can't you?' This was because when we were chatting one day, he dropped his phone and just picked it straight up. I'm like, 'You can fucking see, you bastard.' And he goes, 'What do you mean?' And I'm like, 'Mate, you didn't even feel around. No hesitation.' And he goes, 'Nah, it's the Spidey senses.'

Strictly – and the jungle – changed everything for Sam and me. Because more people got to see who we actually were.

Sam

Before all that, we had this really loyal little crew, people who'd followed us for years. But those two shows brought in a whole new audience, people who didn't know us at all, found the pod, and went, 'Fuck, these two are actually funny.'

Pete

It was the first time older viewers saw us for who we were and not the caricature. A lot of them didn't know us as 'the cheat on *TOWIE*' or 'the moron on *MiC*'. They just saw a fun guy in the jungle and a bloke with a dry sense of humour giving it a go on *Strictly*.

That was actually quite nice. There were no preconceptions. Just us.

Sam and I have got completely different fans now. The younger ones? They love Sam. Me? I get mums. Aunties.

Grandmas. Weirdly, though, I've had more men come up to me about *Strictly* than anything else. They were like, 'You're just a fucking bloke. You're a good lad.'

Because it stripped everything else away. It wasn't like, 'He thinks he's something.' It was just, 'He's a bit shit, but he's trying.' And I think people liked that.

As for Sam, they all just used to think, What an annoying twat. And he is. But there's more to him than that. There's a deeper side. And he's not like that all the time. He struggles with stuff, same as anyone else.

Sam

I think us being more open about who we are – but more private about our actual lives – has changed how people see us. Because we're not playing characters any more.

Pete

We're not trying to be the cheat or the divvy. We're just being us. And it turns out ... us is all right.

MY DOG SHOW WAS ALL ME. IT HAS MY NAME ON IT, BUT EVEN WITHOUT ME, IT'S A BRILLIANT SHOW

Pete

I don't think *Strictly* had as big an impact on me as the jungle did for Sam. Or maybe I just didn't notice it as much. With those sorts of things, I don't get overwhelmed. But still, I did feel like people's opinions shifted a bit. Not like Pete-o-mania or anything dramatic. It was more subtle than that.

Just the other day, some bloke walking his dog came up to me, shook my hand and went, 'People love what you do, man.' And it was just ... nice. Ten years ago that same guy probably would've called me a fucker. So for someone to go, 'Yeah mate, you seem all right,' it's just decent.

Look, deep down, I don't think I'm a terrible person. And I suppose it's been nice for people to maybe understand me a bit better. My sense of humour, the way I carry myself, all of it.

As it turns out, it was *For Dogs' Sake* that had the biggest impact, probably even more than *Strictly*. The reactions were overwhelming. I had wanted to do a show like that because of my love for dogs, a passion that started when I was ten years old. That's when my mum finally gave in and let us adopt a rescue dog named Arnie.

Our bond was instantaneous. Overnight, I had a best friend, and Arnie found love, trust and consistency with me. We navigated life together. From that moment on, I was determined to do something to help animals in need. I got involved in campaigns to help rescue dogs from a South Korean meat farm and fur farms in Finland, and I've supported different animal welfare campaigns – including Lucy's Law, which was passed to put an end to the cruel trade of puppy farming in England. I am also the patron of the charity Dogs On The Streets, which provides support to homeless people and their dogs.

I'm glad to say that South Korea has recently banned the raising, slaughtering and sales of dogs for consumption, with the law coming into effect in 2027

As I've often said, I prefer dogs to people. They have transformed my life for the better, and I'm committed to doing everything I can for them.

I'd always said, if I was ever going to do one thing on TV, that would be it. That's what I care about. I'd already done loads of stuff with dog charities, but back then, no one really wanted to give you a show for that. No one cared what a Z-list nobody thought about dogs. Still, I kept pitching it, year after year. No one wanted it. And as this book has shown, it took a long time for me to truly find my footing and become relevant. Only then were we able to get the project off the ground. I literally finished filming the first series of *For Dogs' Sake* and the next day started *Strictly*.

While I was dancing like a dickhead, the dog show was

being edited in the background, and it aired straight after *Strictly* ended. That whole period was the most nervous I've ever been. Because that show was all me. It has my name on it, but even without me, it's a brilliant show. And that's what I'm proud of.

The show was really well received, and the channel were over the moon with the ratings. Smashed their records, in fact. The first series won a Broadcast Award. I never expected that. And I reckon a big part of it was people who found me on *Strictly* thinking, I'll give that a go – he seems all right.

What made me most proud was the impact the show had on viewers. Lots of people were inspired to look into taking on a dog, while the Dogs Trust centre in Basildon, where we filmed a segment, revealed that after the show aired they'd seen homing enquiries and footfall shoot up by 40 per cent and enquiries about volunteering rising by 50 per cent. I mean, what more could I ask for? That was what the show was about.

A few years earlier I had written a book about dogs, with some of the money going to charity. Bit niche, bit factual, but I loved it. I did it for me, and I did it for the cause. People who've followed me for a while know I've been doing animal stuff for years. But this show finally joined the dots between that passion and what I do for work.

Now I've got a second and third series commissioned. And guess what? I'm associate producer on it. So I'm not just fronting it, I'm really involved. That means something to me. It's rare I say I'm proud of anything I've done. But that? That's one of them. And our award-winning podcast. And even though it hasn't worked out yet, I still rate that sitcom idea we had.

Sam
See Pete, you're bloody awesome. You were made for TV, even if you don't think you are.

Pete

But being in front of the camera isn't something I see myself doing long term.

Sam

Pete, you must! And you will, if I have my way.

Pete

It's partly because of the receding hairline. Mostly because I'm just getting older. But I've found I like creating meaningful telly. Stuff that might actually make a bit of a difference. Aside from the ratings, the impact that dog show had on Dogs Trust was incredible. If we can do that again – even a little bit – that makes me happy.

Hand on heart, it's the first time in ten years of being on telly that I've felt like I've got an actual job. Not just being paid to be me. I feel like I'm doing some good. I hosted a Dogs Trust fundraiser at the Kennel Club in London back in the summer, along with Kirsty Gallacher, who asked me about my experience as a Dogs Trust ambassador – along with the King, if you fucking please – and *For Dogs' Sake*. On the night, one lady paid £40k for a selfie with me, then donated another £40k ten minutes later for another one. So that was £80k in ten minutes. Amazing.

Sam

Mate, you are smashing it.

Pete

When Sam did *I'm a Celeb*, I took a step back from the 'us' stuff. I went into build mode. Behind the scenes, I was laying foundations, writing, pushing the podcast, thinking long-term.

Sam

People started saying, 'Look at Pete Wicks.' Not just a shouty bloke on reality TV, but someone doing something.

Pete

It's a small world, so word gets around. And I reckon that shift came from two years of not just saying yes to any old job. I started being selective, started planning, and in that time, Sam took centre stage. And rightly so.

Sam

At the start of this book you said that you didn't like telly and that you didn't have a proper job or know what you wanted to do. But look at you now. You're writing our tour, you run your own company, you're exec-producing a successful TV show, you're hosting a successful men's mental health podcast ... And it's flying. Pete, you're fucking awesome.

Pete

I guess maybe I am beginning to find my path. After ten fucking years, it's about time. I felt like I was just drifting. Wandering about, doing stuff, wondering if any of it meant anything. Maybe I do have an idea what I want. Or maybe I'm still just blagging it and will one day get bored and turn my back on it, and go and live in the mountains with a herd of goats.

Sam

With me by your side.

Pete

No chance. Just me, the dogs and a bunch of goats. But for now, I'm invested in *Staying Relevant* and our business. This industry is not easy. Keeping momentum, keeping things going – it's exhausting. Then suddenly I feel like I'm getting somewhere. And that's a good feeling. I treat it like a business now. Because I am one. A shit one, maybe, but still a business.

It might be a bit harder for Sam, because doing the jungle was a pinnacle for him. That was the dream. What comes next? How can he top *that*?

THE BUZZ COMES FROM CREATING SOMETHING OUT OF NOTHING

Sam

Pete's right: the jungle was the dream, but it also was a turning point for me. When I was in there, I said to myself, I'd like to try different things. I wanted to take a slightly different path as I'd managed to make inroads into shows that I had only ever dreamed of – like presenting on *This Morning*, or appearing on *Loose Men*, *Celebrity Gladiators* and *Celebrity Sabotage*. Whatever comes next, whether I smash it or fall flat, it's something new. And I am happy with that.

And you know what? Now I know what I want to do. What I love more than anything is creating stuff. That's where my heart is. I want to make great telly, I want to make really fun Instagram ads, I want to do cool stuff – whether it's podcasts or radio or whatever. That's what makes me happy. In 2025 I launched an app with my co-founder Ben, called Content Jungle, a platform where top brands, creators and talent can discover each other and unite to create truly incredible work and projects. And it's not all digital stuff: I even created the sunglasses brand Dinelli with one of my best mates, Rez. We started very small, but then demand really took off. We absolutely love what we've created, and there's no buzz like seeing a pair of Dinelli sunglasses on someone out and about!

The buzz for me comes from creating something out of nothing. That's where I come alive. Pete's the business man.

Pete
Ain't that the fucking truth!

Sam
Pete's in charge of all that.

Pete
Yeah, I handle the business side. I'm the adult.

Sam
And I just, well, irritate him. And that's why we work so well together.

Pete
Yep, that's on his CV – reality moron and celebrity irritant.

Sam
But honestly, I trust him with that stuff. I know he's going to look after it. I just want to have fun, I want to make things that people remember. I want to build something that lasts.

I want to grow the production company. I want us to make our own shows. Our own podcasts, our own radio shows. I want divisions! I've got so many ideas for things I want to do with this. It's just the beginning.

And I know I don't care about the numbers side of it, but that's why this partnership with Pete works so well. Because that's exactly where he thrives. That's what he's brilliant at.

Pete
My strengths are his weaknesses, and vice versa. At different points in our careers, one of us has taken the lead, and the other has done something that's helped us both a lot. Sam comes up with the ideas and I do the groundwork and all the rest of it.

Sam

That's part of why I think our friendship has lasted this long. We support each other. We're at different building stages throughout. And that's kind of how this whole TV game works – you have building years.

Pete

When I'm in a building year, Sam's in his full-frontal year, and the other way round. What we always come back to is each other. And the thing we enjoy the most out of everything we do is the stuff we do together, even though we grow individually.

Sam

No one works together as well as we work together. I genuinely believe that.

That's the secret to a good partnership, right? You come at it from two different angles. You look after different parts. If there's too much overlap, you end up getting in each other's way. But us? We stay in our lanes. And that's why it works.

27

The Importance of Having Proper Mates

Sam

I don't have that many showbiz friends. Weirdly, neither does Pete. The ones I do have, they're just actual friends, which is lovely. Like Marvin and Tony – we went through something real together, and we bonded over it. Tony is just a good guy. He's so solid – a proper mate. He's there for his pals through thick and thin. Pete loves him. Marvin too – he's always there for his friends. His family's beautiful. They welcome you in so warmly. And none of it's about showbiz. I don't film content with Tony and Marvin really. I obviously film with Pete. But I'm really selective – these are real friends.

Pete

Yeah, I can count my mates on one hand. I can say hi to people I meet at parties and on the telly, but they're not proper mates. I wouldn't cry on their shoulder at two in the morning.

Sam

I don't actually believe in showbiz friends. I don't even know what that means. If they're your friends, they're your actual friends. I've got a really small circle. My circle is literally: my sister and Ryan, Marvin, Tony and Pete. I don't need anything more than that. There are also friends from the past who I still hang out with, and they all fit so well into that little circle.

I've always been drawn to people with something about them. Pete, Tony, Marvin – they're all macho geezers with hearts of gold. Sometimes they don't show that side, and I like to bring it out. I find them interesting. They've got so much humour in them.

Liv Attwood is obviously very close to Pete. I love that. Me and Pete see enough of each other for it to actually be a blessing when someone else takes him off my hands for a while. But I get along with his mates so well. They're all such legends. I love them. He's simply not going to be friends with wankers – that's one thing I can always count on. Whoever Pete is friends with, I know I'm going to get along with them. Whether they get along with me is a different story.

My professional circle is also very small, but I trust them 100 per cent. Seb and Jonny from Insanity, my management, always steer me in the right direction and are just great guys. They work closely with Pete's managers Gemma and Ellen. Pete and I share the same publicists, Charlotte and Megan at Belle PR, who are always there for us among the chaos we bring!

Both Pete and I purposely keep our professional team small, but we trust them implicitly and they all get on so well. We are really lucky to have such good people around us, personally and professionally.

Why I love Marvin Humes

Marv is honestly one of the most grounded, lovely blokes I've ever met. You see him on TV and think, He's a pop star, he's a presenter, he's mates with everyone, and it's true, he is all those things. But when you actually hang out with him, you realise he's just a normal lad. He never acts like he's above anyone. I remember the first time I properly met him, I was bricking it a bit. I mean, come on, it's Marvin from JLS. And within two minutes he was chatting away, asking me about myself, laughing at my terrible jokes, just making me feel completely at ease.

He's like the calm in the storm, y'know? I'm quite chaotic, I get excited, I overshare, I talk a million miles an hour, and Marvin's just cool. He's got that energy that makes you want to be better just by being around him. Like, he's so professional but never makes you feel small.

And don't even get me started on how good he is at everything. DJ, host, singer – you name it, he smashes it. But he'll never sit there and list his achievements. He's humble to a fault. Plus, he's got this wicked dry sense of humour, proper dad jokes sometimes, but he owns it. I honestly couldn't say a bad word about him. If you're mates with Marv, you're doing life right.

My best mate Vicky Pattison

I've known Vic for over ten years now, and honestly, she's not just a mate: she's family. We've been through the lot together – highs, lows and everything in between. I was flower boy at her wedding. She's one of those rare people who's just there, always. No judgement, no nonsense, just proper love.

We first met doing a PA together in Weston-super-Mare – glamorous, I know. I'd been on *TOWIE* about three weeks, and the venue clearly had some budget left over so they shoved the two of us together. They tried to make us take pictures separately, but no one really wanted one with me so we just teamed up. From that night on, that was it. We got chucked out of the club, went back to the hotel and I pushed her around reception on a luggage trolley until she passed out.

She's one of the only people who can make me open up, really open up, and manages to do it without me even realising. And she's a crier. When I had her on *Man Made*, she started bawling about thirty seconds in and didn't stop.

She's proper clever. She speaks so well, she's so honest, so sharp, and that's why she's not just one of my best friends but one of the people I admire most. She's had a mad journey, especially when it comes to relationships and how she views men, and honestly, what she has to say is important. People need to hear it. She's seen all sides of me – good, bad and absolutely chaotic – and she's always stuck around. That's rare. She's one of the best people I know.

Why I love Tony Bellew

Tony is so much like Pete it's scary. I always say they are cut from the same cloth.

Tony's got this exterior – you see him, and he looks terrifying, right? I mean, he's a former world champion boxer, he's got that don't-even-think-about-it look. But as soon as you get talking to him, you realise he's got the biggest heart going. Loyalty means something to him, like proper loyalty, not the fake, fair-weather stuff.

And the banter is unreal. Tony's got a really dry, sarcastic, blink-and-you-miss-it sense of humour, and Pete's exactly the same. Half the time you're thinking, Is he joking or is he actually about to tell me off? and then he cracks a little smile and you're like, Ah, right, yeah, I'm safe.

What's mad is how both of them have this rough, rugged exterior, but deep down they're big soft lads. They're the type who pretend they don't care but are secretly the first ones checking in on you when they know you're going through something. And when you listen to Tony talk about his fights, his family, his upbringing, it's just like Pete when he opens up. It's raw, it's real, it's proper life experience.

If Pete had a Scouse twin, it'd be Tony Bellew. Same moral code, same loyalty, same don't mess with the people I care about attitude, and underneath it all, a heart of absolute gold. Two of the realest blokes you'll ever meet.

Why I tolerate Olivia Attwood

So here's how it goes. Me and Liv, we've been mates for about five years. And the way we've kept it going that long is pretty simple: I find her physically repulsive. No attraction, no drama. Just solid friendship built on mutual insults and getting hammered together. A bit tragic, but it works.

We met after she came off *Love Island*, sitting next to each other at some random event. Liv started slagging off her ex about half an hour in, we got properly drunk, took the piss out of everyone around us, and weirdly that night turned into a five-year friendship where we've just carried on insulting each other. Beautiful, really.

Later on, she joined *TOWIE* at a time when I wasn't enjoying it as much as I had been. She was a whirlwind, turned up on set, loud as you like, and gave me a fun reason to keep going.

We're unapologetically ourselves. Always have been. That's why people either love us or absolutely despise us. No in-between. And that's fine – we're not here for validation. We're here for a laugh, some honesty, and the odd brand deal if we're lucky. Of course, we also have our own weekly radio show together on Kiss, aptly titled *The Sunday Roast*. It's basically a couple of hours of me and Liv chatting shit and having a laugh.

We're also good at narrating our own chaos. We mess up, but we'll hold our hands up, laugh about it and move on. No shifting the blame, no crocodile tears. If you're a knob, say you're a knob.

28

Staying Resilient

Like it or not, being famous means you are always being watched by the press. And we are not always happy about it.

Pete

As I've said before, when I started out in this industry I was the villain because of the character I played on *TOWIE*. I was called the lothario, the scruffy love machine who couldn't keep his cock in his trousers. I did a few stupid things, but I wasn't that bad. Though I did play up to, or rather lean into, being the villain to stay relevant. It created headlines, got me noticed by producers who thought I was good telly, so work came out of it. But it was always just me. I didn't care if I was in the paper every week with a different girl. It was all part of the game, trying to make a living in this world.

All the way through, I never manipulated it. I was just careless.

Now? If I'm going on a date I go out of my way to enter separately. Leave separately. Because you've got to respect someone's privacy. You never know how it might work out, and I don't want to drag someone into my world if they don't want to be there.

Looking back, I should have handled things better. I'm at a different age now, with a different mindset. I value privacy more than I ever have. The way I look at dating is different to the way Sam should. He's just a puppy who bounces along, whereas the way I lived my lifestyle back in the day created this monster of a character that has stuck with me ever since.

Sam
The press didn't care about me much until I started going out with my last girlfriend and certain dramas took place in our lives, which played out in the press and also on *MiC*. I even had the press camped outside my house for three weeks. Just sitting there, waiting for me to catch me in a vulnerable state. I know I'm in the public eye, but I think they sometimes forget that I am a human being.

Pete
Yeah, you see, he cares what people think of him. Sam's never really had bad press, not like me. I've had it for years.

I think this is a new era of fame for Sam. Although *Strictly* was good for me, I'm still in the same place I've always been. The narrative hasn't changed much, although I'm perhaps perceived as more credible now.

Sam
I disagree. What with your dog show and your *Man Made* podcast, I think people are seeing the real Peter James Wicks.

Pete
Maybe. I mean, I have been introduced as a 'presenter, podcaster and radio DJ' rather than 'reality star'. So that was a change. I was like, fuck me, I've gone up in the world. That actually sounds like things people do. We're both probably

at that stage now – all these years in – where we're only just starting our careers. Our legitimate careers. Before this, it's been an illegitimate career. Like little bastard careers. You know what I mean?

Sam

What means so much to me is the relationship I share with the people who follow me online. There's no better feeling than when someone messages me saying one of my videos made a crappy day a bit better. That's amazing.

Or when I post an Instagram story saying, 'We're gonna have a great day today,' and I get hundreds of replies like, 'Thanks, Sam. Really needed that.' Pete takes the piss because I do it all the time, but people respond. That means the world to me.

The most important thing, though, are the connections that have come from being open about ADHD and autism, the people who thank me for talking about it. Do you know how much it takes for someone to say that to a stranger? There's so much love out there. I adore it.

Pete

It's easy to get bogged down by the negatives, but if I dropped dead tomorrow I've done more with my life than I ever dreamed of doing. And the best part? I've done most of it with my best mate.

IF SOMEONE TELLS YOU YOU'RE A PIECE OF SHIT ENOUGH TIMES, YOU START TO BELIEVE IT

Pete

Don't get me wrong. I know I moan about what's written about me in the press, but there are a lot of journalists who have been so supportive over the years, when I've appeared on TV shows or I've had a charity to promote. I am eternally grateful to them for their love and support.

The ones who do get on my wick are the handful who seem to go out of their way to hurt people. Not just me. Everyone. Anyone who is the public eye is game. I know it's a job, but I just wish they'd remember that it can be hard to read something negative about yourself. If someone tells you you're a piece of shit enough times, you start to believe it.

Last year, on World Mental Health Day, a story about my mum trying to kill herself hit the headlines. It was based on a section of *Never Enough*, and what hurt me most was that that very personal story that I had been careful to handle with great sensitivity was taken out of context and rehashed for clicks. My mum was in the *Strictly* audience that week, sitting there, watching it all unfold. I never said in my book that my childhood was traumatic. I said my mum attempted suicide, but I never used it for sympathy. I only wrote about it because she's open about it. Because she's my hero. And because people need to hear it. Mental health is a part of life. We all go through shit. Everyone struggles. And sometimes, hearing someone else say 'Yeah, I've been there too,' makes it easier.

That was the point of the last book. To show that even in this ridiculous world I live in, I fucking struggle too. We all do. And if sharing my story helps one person feel like they're not stuck in the hole alone, then it was worth it.

That's why this book we're doing now is meant to be funny, meant to be light-hearted – though maybe we have taken a dark but important turn – but also about showing people that we're just like everyone else. We have struggles. We're absolutely no fucking different from anyone else.

You could work in Tesco or be a billionaire – we all endure struggles. But the thing is, no one thinks or feels or experiences things exactly like you do. That's why it can feel so lonely. That's why telling these stories matters, that's why I wanted to do this book. So people can actually hear our side of things. The truth behind the glitz and the filters and the clickbait. Because it's all just a load of bollocks really, isn't it?

We work hard. We graft. We care. But we also know it's a bit of a joke, and that's fine. As long as we're honest about it.

Shag Marry Kill

We couldn't get through a book without a good-natured round of Shag Marry Kill. For this very special book edition, we asked Staying Relevant *fans to choose some options for us to chew the fat over.*

Round 1: Vicky Pattison, Nigel Farage and Jowita

Pete
I mean, this one's a no-brainer.

Sam
Me too, although he was nice to me in the jungle.

Pete
I'd have to marry Vic. We've been mates for over ten years now. And we're kind of like a married couple. Just without the sex. Which I guess is like marriage.

Sam
And, of course, she's marriage material, as she's already married. So that must mean she'd be good at the marriage thing.

Pete
Which leaves Jowita. So I'd have to shag her. Now, before anyone tries to make out this is an admission of love, it's not! I've chosen her for the purposes of this game, as I ain't gonna play tonsil tennis with Nigel fucking Farage or Vicky, am I? So Jowita it is. Not only is she a lovely girl and one of my best mates, she's flexible. And by that, I mean she's a great dancer.

Sam
And you know what they say about great dancers?

Pete
What? Good rhythm?

Sam
Er, yes, actually.

Round 2: Pat Butcher from *EastEnders*, Ursula from *The Little Mermaid* and Skeletor from *He-Man and the Masters of the Universe*

Pete
Ah, that's a cracking line-up.

Sam
Wait, who's Skeletor?

Pete
The evil villain from the old *He-Man* cartoons – skinny fucker with a skull for a face, always trying to conquer the world. You know, classic little-dick syndrome.

Sam
Right, kill Skeletor. No clue who he is, but if he's trying to take over the universe I'd have to kill him. To save all of mankind. I'm good like that.

Pete
Me too. I'd definitely shag Ursula, because...

Sam
Tentacles everywhere.

Pete
You know what I mean? She could do some serious multi-tasking. She could wank me off with any one of them.

Sam
Yeah, imagine where she puts her tentacles – with all those little suckers too.

Pete
Different tentacles – it'd basically be like being wanked off by eight people at once. Like that old trick where you sit on your hand until it's numb – same sort of idea. And also, she's a bad bitch. Got that villain energy.

Sam
Yeah, totally. She's wicked – like, you wouldn't know what she's going to bring to the table. She'd keep you guessing. And there's a bit of magic going on as well.

Pete
Then I'd marry Pat Butcher. I feel like we'd just have a lovely chilled life together. We'd smoke ourselves into an early grave. I love the leopard print.

Sam
I think I'd have to agree, as boring as that sounds.
   But then, what has Skeletor *actually* done? Are we judging him purely for being a skeleton? Bit unfair, maybe?

Pete
Like I said, he's an evil cunt.

Sam
But we always like to fix someone, try to make them a good person. Like a project. Skeletor could be that project.

Pete
To be honest, we need to be the project, as we need to sort ourselves out.

Sam
Yes, we need to be changed.

Pete
And, come to think of it, I'm not sure if Pat Butcher, Skeletor or Ursula would actually want to shag us.

Sam
I reckon Skeletor doesn't get much.

Pete
But he'd probably still say no.

The Future

WHAT THE FUTURE HOLDS

Pete

So we've reached the end of this book. Thank Christ for that. It took a lot longer than I expected. Now it's time to say goodbye and thank you to everyone who actually made it this far. What an achievement. Before you chuck this book in the swap box at your local supermarket, let Samuel and me take a moment for reflection.

Sam

Yes, let's look ahead to our very exciting future ...

Pete

The future? Fuck me. After this book, do we have a future? Do I even want one?

Sam

Of course you do. What are you looking forward to?

Pete

My first instinct? I've got no idea. I don't even like being famous. If I could just go back to being completely and utterly anonymous, dying a lonely death in a cave, I would.

What I do love about *Staying Relevant* the company

is that I'm doing a bit of writing and working behind the scenes. Slowly, I'm trying to pull myself out from in front of the camera and go behind it. The issue is ... I've got a business partner who lives to be in front of the camera.

Sam
And I'll always try to drag you straight back out there.

Pete
It's like one of those old cartoons in which someone's being dragged offstage with the Little Bo Peep hook. That's me. Only I'm trying to walk off and he's pulling me right back on.

Sam
I reckon we'll be on stage until we're sixty-five years old.

Pete
I'll be dead.

Sam
I don't care. I'll revive you.

Pete
You'll revive me? So if the technology's there, you're gonna electronically pulsate into my dead corpse?

Sam
And then just ... wank.

Pete
You'll what?

Sam
Sorry, that was weird.

Pete
'I'll electronically pulsate into his dead body and wank.' Do you see what I have to put up with?

Sam
When Pete eventually dies, I want to mummify him.

Pete
He wants to fucking taxidermy me.

Sam
Yeah. Taxidermy. Then I'll encase you in resin and make a desk out of you.

Pete
A desk! That's exactly what I want. He'll even have a little area for his pen, which will just be my ...

Sam
... arsehole. No, it'll be a pencil sharpener, and I'll spend all day sharpening my pencils in it. And there will be nothing you can do about it.

Pete
Oh, I will. I'll fucking haunt you until the day you die.

Sam
He'll be looking down at me – or up, knowing him – and going, 'You cunt.'

Pete
What in the Jeffrey Dahmer is happening here?

Sam
If I died first, I've got this vision of Pete in bits, crying at my tombstone, laying flowers, leaning against a tree, completely broken. And then we'd win a posthumous BAFTA.

Pete
No, if Sam died – and I'm being serious here – I would be absolutely gutted. It would probably ruin this whole industry for me. And let's be honest, it's already ruined for me. But the one shining light I have, the one bit I genuinely enjoy, is this prick.

Sam
Aww, mate.

Pete
So if he was gone, there'd be nothing left for me. I'd disappear, buy some land, live with dogs and goats, completely off-grid. You'd never hear from me again.

Now, if I died? Sam's first thought would be to shag my grave like that bloke in *Saltburn*, and then head to Amazon and Netflix to pitch a documentary called *The Man Behind the Eyes*.

Sam
The Sadness Behind the Eyes.

Pete
And if I got cancelled before I died, Sam would run to every network with *The Monster Inside*.

Sam
The Monster Inside: I Always Knew.

Pete

Living With a Monster: Pete Wicks by Sam Thompson. He'd keep it going. He'd say, 'Yeah, it's really sad . . . but also, what a great career opportunity.'

Sam

I feel like the views would be through the roof.

Pete

He'd be on *This Morning, Good Morning Britain*, all of it. Then he'd write a book on grief and launch a show at the O2 called *Pete, Are You There?* Not just one night – a full three-month residency.

Sam

Yes! A show about trying to contact Pete from the other side. I'd have a ouija board and everything.

Pete

On a more serious note, and we should end this book sounding like authors, not two idiotic teenagers, Sam's got big plans for us. He thinks there's still a big break ahead.

Sam

We're going Stateside, baby. We're going shiny-floor.

Pete

If we're not careful, we'll be mopping that shiny floor.

Sam

We're going to land a big Saturday-night show. Maybe a dating show. We're going to be the new TV duo in town. And then I see us flying – not going by boat – to the States.

Pete

Fairly realistic, that. I see us on a plane and then ...

Sam

And then we're in LA. I honestly think we'll spend a year out there at some point. We'll have loads of meetings and we'll land our own shiny-floor chat show.

Pete

The only thing we're making in America is smoothies, out the back of a truck.

Sam

And if we are? Fine, we'll turn that into content, baby. I don't care.

Pete

But Sam, what if the fame fades? What if we become has-beens?

Sam

You'd move on.

Pete

Damn right I would.

Sam

But I'd fight tooth and nail. You know what's great about this industry now? No one's in charge. Everyone has the chance to take control of their destiny. I love that. I'll just keep doing the podcast with Pete, keep making stuff, and keep going after our shiny-floor American dream, even if we're seventy years old.

Pete

Serious question . . . Are we in this for life?

Sam

We're in it for life. 100 per cent.

Pete

Why are we in it for life? Is it the fame?

Sam

Oh, we're definitely in the fame game for life.

Pete

Are you in it for life? I'm still not sure I am.

Sam

I am! And here's why: the things I love doing all run parallel with the fame game. I love this industry. Genuinely. I love presenting, interviewing, making videos, podcasting, all of it. And all of that needs an audience. I've always loved entertaining people. When the audience likes it, that's the best feeling in the world. You know those messages we get when someone says, 'That video of you dicking Pete against the wall in the Spider-Man costume made my day'? That's what it's all about. It's fun. We're not taking ourselves seriously. It's all good energy and lightness – and if I can do that every day with my best mate, then fuck yeah, I want it for ever.

Despite what Pete thinks, fame isn't the goal. The goal is doing the stuff I love, with the person I love doing it with. And fame just happens to come with that.

Pete

Wow! It only took you eighty thousand words to finally say something intelligent. And, fuck me, I can't believe

I'm saying this, but I agree. I could do without the fame. I actively despise it. But what I do love is being able to make a difference now and then. If we make one person smile, we've done our job. And I love that I get to do this with my best mate. So yeah, if that means I've got to take the dogshit side of fame just to live this life with someone I actually want to live it with, then I'll take it.

Sam

That's exactly what I want to do. For ever. As long as we can. Until Pete dies.

Acknowledgements

Thank you to our *Staying Relevant* listeners. Without you there would be no podcast and no book. You have made our dreams come true.

To our Staying Relevant Productions team. Producer Pippa, Josh, TV Ted, Annalise, Hannah, Kiera and Gurlina. The best in the business.

To our brilliant personal and professional teams. Gemma, Ellen and Team Mokkingbird. Seb, Jonny and Team Insanity. Charlotte, Megan and Team Belle PR. We'd be lost without you.

To the Little, Brown team for believing in *Staying Relevant* THE BOOK – we've done it!

To Christian for putting our chaos, words and stories on paper – that's no easy task!

To Duncan for designing and creating our brilliant avatars.

To Jo Bell – you are the best. This book wouldn't exist without your hard work and dedication. What shall we write next?

And to our families and friends.

You know who you are.
We love you.

Stay Relevant.

Sam and Pete
x